Matthew M. Vriends, Ph.D.

HAND-FEEDING AND RAISING
BABY BIRDS

Breeding, Hand-feeding, Care, and Management

With Illustrations by Tanya M. Heming-Vriends
and 98 Photographs by Famous Bird Photographers

BARRON'S

Dedication

For Tanya, Kimy, and Eddie and Robbin L. McNeill, with love

Soyons fidèles à nos faiblesses.

Experience is a wonderful thing. It enables you to recognize a mistake when you make it again.

All inquiries should be addressed to:
Barron's Educational Series, Inc.
250 Wireless Boulevard
Hauppauge, New York 11788

International Standard Book No. 0-8120-9581-2

Library of Congress Catalog Card No. 96-3189

Library of Congress Cataloging-in-Publication Data
Vriends, Matthew M., 1937–
    Hand-feeding and raising baby birds : breeding, hand-feeding, care, and management / Matthew M. Vriends ; with illustrations by Tanya M. Heming-Vriends.
        p.   cm.
    Includes bibliographical references (p.) and index.
    ISBN 0-8120-9581-2
    1. Cage birds. 2. Cage birds—Infancy. I. Title.
SF461.V729   1996
636.6'8—dc20   96-3189
                                                     CIP

Printed in Hong Kong

98765432

About the Author

Matthew M. Vriends, the author of this book, is a Dutch-born biologist/ornithologist who holds a collection of advanced degrees, including a Ph.D. in zoology. Dr. Vriends has written over a hundred books in three languages on birds, mammals, and other animals. Well known are his detailed works on lovebirds, Australian parakeets, and finches. Dr. Vriends has traveled extensively in South America, the United States, Indonesia, Africa, Australia, and Europe to observe and study birds in their natural environment and is widely regarded as an expert in tropical ornithology and aviculture. Dr. Vriends is the author or advisory editor of many of Barron's pet books. For his daughter Tanya, a graduate from the University of Cincinnati, *Hand-feeding and Raising Baby Birds* is the fourth book she illustrated for her father.

Photo Credits

Patrick Vaernewyck: front cover, inside back cover, back cover; J. G. Blasman: inside front cover, pages 2 top and bottom, 3 top and bottom, 10, 13 top and bottom, 14 top and bottom, 15 top and bottom, 16 top and bottom, 24 bottom left, 25, 26, 27, 28 top, 29 top, 30 bottom, 31 top left, top right, bottom right, 33 bottom left, bottom right, 35 top and bottom, 42, 43, 53, 55, 63, 68, 71, 72 top and bottom, 73 top and bottom, 74, 75, 76 top and bottom, 78, 79, 80, 99 top and bottom, 100 top and bottom, 103, 104, 106 top and bottom, 107 top and bottom; Dr. Matthew M. Vriends: pages 17 left and right, 24 top left and top right, 28 bottom, 29 bottom left and bottom right, 30 top, 36, 40, 58, 101, 108 top, 112, 113, 119, 120, 127, 128, 129, 131; B. Everett Webb: pages 33 top right, 87 left and right, 91, 97, 108 bottom, 121, top, 126 top and bottom; Joan Balzarini: pages 92, 109, 110 top and bottom, 111; Carlton Gower: pages 34, 44, 45, 121 bottom, 122, 123, 125, 140

Preface

The export of birds and other animals destined for the pet trade in the United States and Western European countries is being increasingly banned by many of the countries of origin. At one stage there were even concerns that our country's pet bird boom was about to go bust, but, on the contrary, the lack of imported, frequently shy and noisy wild birds has quickly made way for artificially incubated, patiently and lovingly (at least in most cases) hand-reared birds. The demand for these domestically raised birds is ever-increasing, due to the fact that they usually retain their babylike characteristics, and are thus more attractive and petlike, than their "uncivilized," screaming wild ancestors.

If you had entered a bird room a few years ago, you would have frequently seen (and in some cases you still see) a number of young parrots exhibited in old aquarium tanks, being busily hand-fed by the aviculturists. Even at bird shows it was not uncommon to see baby parrots, sometimes only a few days old, sitting on decrepit, dirty old towels, the birds retching from the effect of the hashed up mixture of such items as peanut butter and monkey chow! Some hand-feeders were so fervent in their actions that they tried to feed, in lightning tempo, five or six birds at a time with a syringe. I have often asked myself: "How many losses does this 'hasty' feeding lead to?" And "Is the love of money, rather than the love of birds the driving force?"

Fortunately, this impulsive rearing of large numbers of pet parrots has somewhat abated and hand-rearers today take a more professional, loving, and feeling attitude. Oh yes, you still hear the opinion that "the more youngsters the better," but there is little we can do about it; remember, puppy mills are indeed still a thorn in the eye of every animal lover—but they still flourish!

The conscientious fanciers and breeders are steadily gaining more ground. They are convinced that hand-raising baby birds is mostly a labor of love, coupled with great dedication and much loss of sleep! One knows that hand-feeding involves a great deal of research, forethought, and planning. Various equipment, tools, and techniques are required to stay in front, and one should not take the attitude (as I once heard at a big bird show) that "there is a tube to fit in every

Contents

beak." The real fancier knows well that certain species can be successfully reared only with professional techniques. There are trials and tribulations in raising and hand-feeding baby birds!

At first it may appear to be quite uncomplicated. Various hand-feeding diets are available on the market. These are mixed to the correct consistency and temperature in hot clean water, following the manufacturer's instructions. Using a syringe (also available in pet shops), a tube, or a "bent" spoon, the mixture is fed to the baby. That's it? No, nothing in life goes quite so easily as that! Of course, many baby birds, especially parrots, are quite resilient and quickly adapt to the environment and to the hands that feed them. In no time they will regard the person who feeds them as their parent, but however willing the bird is to allow you to feed it, a number of diseases and difficulties can always rear their ugly heads, like slow crop, crop burn, sour crop, stress, yeast infections, dehydration and regurgitation, to name but a few (see Chapter 9, Health Problems)! What do we do about these?

This book approaches hand-feeding and everything that goes directly and indirectly with it, primarily from the practical side. I have been an avid aviculturist for some 40 years, so I can draw on considerable practical experience. While my own background contributes to the major part of the text, I have also brought in the parallel experiences of many aviculturist friends throughout the world. Not long ago, a review of one of my books stated that "Vriends is interested only in breeding birds" and, indeed, I do get a great deal more pleasure doing this than, for example, teaching a cockatoo how to roller-skate. It is ironic that the writer of that statement is now editor of a bird magazine that carries the word "breeder" in its title! Indeed, I have always been very interested in the breeding of cage and aviary birds; hence, it is my intent here, to be more practical than scientific. I am aware that, biologist that I am, I have not resisted adding a paragraph or two that, strictly speaking, is not essential to the practical side of raising birds. I hope these extra insights add to the reader's general knowledge and enjoyment. That is why, as well as discussing artificial incubation in an incubator, I also pay attention to natural incubation, if only to hold the natural instincts of the parents. Additionally, the discussions on natural incubation will be useful for those fanciers who do not have an incubator, but in certain emergencies may have to attempt to save a hatchling from certain death; the knife cuts both ways!

In the text of this volume, I have given considerable space to the hookbills, many of which are now endangered species. I believe that, as aviculturists, we can and will play a very important role in the preservation of these and other endangered avian species. I don't mean to show any personal preference to the parrots and parakeets, even though I dwell on them at length; this emphasis is generated more or less out of necessity. Extensive attention is also devoted to budgerigars and cockatiels, since they are far and away the most popular pet birds in out country.

I don't make a claim to absolute wisdom! When I present my way of raising young, I don't mean to say this is the only way, or the only good way. The text that follows is completely subject to any valid corrections and additions, which may become necessary.

I hope this book can make a contribution, small as it may be, to the preservation of our natural environment, which is being threatened from all sides. I believe that the serious bird owner and breeder is no threat to the survival of birds in nature in any part of the world—no matter what many bird and animal protectionists say. In fact, the opposite is true. Efforts of serious aviculturists in the past few years have saved a number of bird species from total extinction. Various other projects (Red-fronted Macaw, Great Green Macaw, Brazilian Cardinal, Red Siskin, and especially the Thick-billed Parrot, among many others) are in progress at this very moment. These are observations well worth making!

Let us then be informed participants in a creative effort that will and should be dynamic. Good luck!

Matthew M. Vriends
Cincinnati, Ohio
Winter 1995/1996

Acknowledgments

I am indebted to the many aviculturists and ornithologists who replied so helpfully to my requests for information, especially Mrs. Robbin L. McNeill of W. Jefferson, N.C., Mrs. Elizabeth Milnar of Ann Arbor, Michigan, Drs. Bob Dalhausen, MS, DVM of Cincinnati, Ohio, and Sam Vaughn, BS, DVM of Louisville, Kentucky. My grateful thanks are due to Mr. John Coborn, Nanango, Queensland, Australia, for his invaluable suggestions, extensive annotations and assistance in many matters concerning this book. I would also like to thank Mr. J. P. Holsheimer, Deventer, The Netherlands, for his ready help in many matters relating to this book.

Thanks to my daughter, Mrs. Tanya M. Heming-Vriends, for her invaluable assistance during the preparation of the text; without her this book could never have been written. Last, but not least, I would like to thank Mr. Michael N. Tuller, editor at Barron's Educational Series Inc., who painstakingly put it all together. All the opinions and conclusions expressed in the following pages are my own, however, and any errors must be my own responsibility.

M.M.V.

Chapter One
From Egg to Hatchling, an Introduction

The Ancestors

One of the most important characteristics of birds is that they lay eggs, an attribute they have inherited from their reptilian ancestors. In the world of mammals there are two species that do not bring living young into the world, the Duck-billed Platypus (*Ornithorhynchus paradoxus [anatinus]*)—in itself a very interesting name—and the Spiny Anteater, or Echidna (*Echidna [Tachyglossus] aculeata [aculeatus]*). These two most primitive of mammals have many unique and interesting features. Certain characteristics are similar to those of reptiles: Both species lay large, leathery-shelled eggs, but both species differ in the ways the eggs are incubated. The Duck-billed Platypus incubates its eggs in a special, vegetation-lined underground chamber. The tiny hatchlings are nurtured on a milklike fluid that exudes from pores in the breast and belly of the mother. She lies on her back so that the fluid runs in drops from her belly and can be licked up by the young. There are no teats on which the young can suck, as is the case with all of the higher mammals.

The female Spiny Anteater doesn't brood its single egg, but carries it in a special pouch situated on her belly. The hatchling is raised on a milky fluid that exudes from pores within her pouch.

Most reptiles, and all bird species are *ovoviviparous* or egg laying, in contrast to the *viviparous* animals that give birth to living young. Some animals are termed *oviparous*—laying single-celled eggs that are fertilized after being

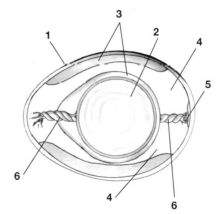

The Egg
1. Shell over two membranes
2. Germ cell and yolk
3. Outer and inner liquid
4. Albumen
5. Air chamber
6. Chalaza

Zebra Finches will breed, if you let them, all year-round, with an average of 4 eggs, although 8 are not unusual.

A fair number of reptile species are viviparous, including the Viviparous Lizard (*Lacerta vivipara*) of Europe, the Slow Worm (*Anguis fragilis*), also of Europe, and the Common Garter Snake (*Thamnophis sirtalis*) of North America.

To summarize, we can say: Neither the ancestors of the birds, the reptiles, nor the descendants of the reptiles, the mammals, have uniform methods of reproduction. There are egg-laying mammals, and there are live-bearing reptiles, but *all* birds lay eggs!

laid (fish and sea urchins, for example) or while being laid (frogs, many insects). Being ovoviviparous, most reptiles and all birds lay eggs that have been fertilized within the maternal body and the embryo has begun to develop well before the eggs are deposited.

The hen Peach-faced Lovebird lays 4 to 5 eggs. After 30 to 38 days, the young fly out of the nest, but will continue to be fed (mostly by the father) for some time.

The Eggshell

The eggshell, which originates in the uterus of the female bird, is made up mainly from calcium carbonate ($CaCO_3$) and other minerals (including phosphorus, manganese, and magnesium), and offers excellent protection for the developing embryo.

With a cursory inspection the shell appears to have a smooth surface, but in reality it is full of pores, made up as a result of the imperfect packing of the calcium crystals. (A chicken's egg contains about 7,000 pores!) Microscopic examinations of eggshells have shown that the number of pores gradually increases from the pointed to the blunt end of the egg. Dr. A. Romanoff (in *The Avian Egg*. New York; John Wiley and Sons, 1949) examined 795 eggs from 260 chickens and discovered an average of 149 pores per square centimeter at the blunt end, compared to only 90 at the pointed end. The pores help absorb moisture and oxygen, and allow escape of carbon dioxide. The membrane inside the shell (see page 21) does not have pores but the gas exchange takes place in the same way as it does in the cells of plants and animals, by *osmosis* (the diffusion of fluid through a semipermeable membrane until there is an equal concentration of fluid on either side of the membrane. In the egg this is an exchange of gases).

The bird's egg can be regarded as a self-contained life-support system. Everything that is necessary for the development of the embryo is available in the egg. As long as the egg gets the correct temperature and oxygen, all elements are available for a positive development.

Color

The color of the eggshell is very variable, even among eggs from the same clutch. We must assume that the eggs of the earliest birds, which died out many millions of years ago, were white with no markings. Many modern species have retained the primitive type. For example, parrots and parakeets, woodpeckers, owls, doves, weavers, Zebra Finches, Gouldians, and many swallows do not require their eggs to be camouflaged as, with a few exceptions (turtledoves, short-eared owls, and eagle owls for example) they are, at least partly, hole-breeders. More-

Five-day-old Gouldian Finches. In the wild, Gouldians construct their nests entirely from grasses and they are dome-shaped. Note the glossy opal shade of the white eggs.

over, white eggs are laid by some large birds such as storks, and many birds-of-prey (White-tailed Sea Eagle, Short-toed Eagle), which have no natural enemies and can afford to have white eggs.

Two-day-old Forpus chicks. The Celestial parrotlet lays 4 to 6 eggs that she incubates for 17 to 21 days.

3

Of course, all of these "white" eggs are not necessarily pure white; some may be chalky-white or yellowish white, others bluish or greenish white. The colors of some eggshells may be environmentally influenced after they are laid. Grebes (*Podicipedidae*) lay chalky-white eggs in a very damp nest that is composed of partially submerged, rotting vegetation. The influence of humus dyes from the rotting vegetation very soon colors the eggs reddish to dark brown. The chemical composition of the water can also affect coloration of eggshells; iron in the water, for example, can give a reddish brown tint. But there are still other birds whose eggs change color. The eggs of the Gray Lag Goose (*Anser anser*) are at first cream-colored, but are soon colored gray, sometimes with brown and yellow blotches, by the action of the nest material. Many raptors have the habit of bringing fresh twigs to the nest. If these are wet, they can stain the eggs with various dyes.

The greatest variation among the unmarked eggs is in the blue and green range. The blue and the green come in every imaginable shade, from the deepest blue (ibises), to pale blue-green (herons, thrushes, bluebirds, various warblers, etc.), or to the soft greenish blue of the blue grosbeak. The blue tint also occurs on the eggs of various hole- and halfhole-breeders, such as starlings, white-eyes (*Zosteropidae*), various sparrows (for example, the Yellow-throated Rock Sparrow, *Gymnorhis flavicollis*, and *Sporophila* species).

A number of bird species lay eggs that fluctuate in color between white and blue respectively green, and between white and yellow respectively brown. Pheasants and nightingales, for example, lay olive-green eggs; many small songbirds lay eggs that are mahogony or terracotta-colored, while some South American tinamous (*Tinamidae*) lay highly glossed deep-chocolate-colored eggs.

Other groups of birds lay marked eggs; these include most raptors, plovers, gulls, and many songbirds. The ground colors come in every possible tint—brown, sand-colored, reddish, green, and blue. The great range of colors is astounding! Even among the eggs of a single species, the ground color and markings can be very variable. You need only look at the egg clutches in a colony of black-headed gulls (*Larus ridibundus*) to see every tint, from the darkest brown to the lightest beige.

We could say that the various eggshells exhibit a veritable carnival of colors, but they all stem from just two kinds of pigment. The first is the greenish blue or blue pigment[1] that occurs in the whole eggshell (that is why the shell can vary from white to

---

[1] These are the so-called *oöcyanines*, which come from bile secretions. Important oöcyanines are blue oöcyanine, yellow oöchlorine and reddish purple oöxantine.

light blue); the second pigment[2] is variable-tinted and can appear as red, brown, or black, and all of the intermediate shades. Dr. Colin Harrison (in *A Field Guide to the Nests, Eggs and Nestlings of North American Birds*, New York: William Collins and Sons Co., Ltd., 1978) states about this pigment: "When it tints the whole shell it is normally only present in the thin surface covering. For example, small quantities of superficial ground color make the white shell appear yellow or buff and the blue shell green or olive. This pigment also produces the shell markings. In the gamebirds such markings are present only on the surface with the superficial tint, but in most other families these markings are applied at intervals as the shell is formed and occur at varying depths within the shell. The shell, being partly translucent, and when in very thin layers partly transparent, means that markings such as these show through a thin layer of shell if near the surface. Markings that are black, red or brown may appear gray, pink or buff, in varying degrees of paleness according to their depth, on white shells; and if the shell is blue may appear in shades of purple, lilac and mauve."

Temperature and Humidity Maintenance

At the beginning of this section we saw that the pores in the eggshell allow the escape of carbon dioxide and water vapor. Under certain conditions—for example, when the egg is very damp, or is suddenly cooled dramatically—it is possible for bacteria and other microscopic organisms to enter through the pores and pose a danger to the developing embryo. It is therefore very important to maintain the correct temperature and humidity during artificial incubation (see pages 69–79) as well as to ensure the highest standards of hygiene.

Finally, I would like to relate a typical remark from a biologist: The eggshell consists not only of a single layer; there are in fact three. The outer, spongy layer, known as the *cuticle*, is composed of keratin fibers and dry mucus, and is, one can say, responsible for the glossy appearance of some eggs. Take, for example, those of a sparrow, or those chocolate-brown, dark gray, or reddish gray eggs of tinamous, which shine like porcelain. The functions of the cuticle are to regulate evaporation of moisture through the shell, but also to prevent the invasion of bacteria and other microorganisms. Beneath the cuticle lies the calcified layer (*testa*), which we know as the eggshell, and under that is the third layer, the mammilary layer that

[2]Here we are concerned with the so-called *oöporfyzines* which occur in hemoglobin. They give a uniform basic color to the eggshell. A white egg lacks any color pigments and the "white" is caused by the calcium. If pigment occurs only on the outer shell, the inside is still white. If the pigment is cast at the same time as the calcium, the eggshell will be similarly colored both inside and out.

consists of roughly hemispherical knobs. Before we look *inside* the egg, we will first make a few remarks with regard to eggshell damage.

Eggshell Repair

Various factors contribute to the damage of eggs in the nest or in the incubator. In natural nests, the eggs can be damaged by parent birds with excessively long nails (puncturing the shell). Unexpected disturbances (sudden nest inspection, sudden loud noise, aggression from other birds, etc.) can cause brooding birds to leave the nest hastily and, in so doing, cause the eggs to bang together and possibly end up with small dents and cracks. Understandably, damaged eggs have little or no chance of producing healthy chicks. Lightly damaged eggs, however, can be saved by repairing them.

I will deal with eggs in which only the shell is damaged, and the egg membrane (see page 21) has remained intact with no punctures or cuts. Serious damage, where a great loss of moisture has occurred, will make the egg unsuitable for incubation as the embryo will soon die!

Before repairing an eggshell, the damaged area and its surroundings should be cleaned up with distilled water and a sterile pad or tissue. Invading bacteria and fungi frequently cause the death of the embryo.

Repairs can be made with paraffin wax (my favorite), nail polish, various nontoxic "school" glues, pieces of gauze or tissue, or pieces of eggshell (from infertile eggs, for example). Even sterile pieces of shell from quail or bantams can sometimes be used (see also page 43).

Hairline Cracks

These are best repaired with Elmer's Glue (or a similar water-soluble, nontoxic "school" glue). Somewhat larger cracks will require several coats of glue; I wait about 30 minutes between each coat. It is highly recommended to weigh each egg as soon as possible after it has been laid (see page 2), so that one can calculate how much weight a damaged egg may have lost. If it is as much as 25 percent, the egg must be carefully monitored during its incubation.

Indentations

When birds suddenly leave the nest in panic, it is quite possible for eggs to bang against each other and cause dents. There are also other causes of such dents. Providing the egg membrane is intact, the repair is similar to that described above: "Fill" with two or three layers of Elmer's Glue. The prepared area can also be covered with a piece of shell from an infertile egg. This method works especially well with larger eggs, such as those from quails or pheasants. With parakeet eggs, I place a piece of sterile gauze (found in every first aid kit) over the damage, after the first layer of glue. If a repair is carried out over the area of the air cell (at the blunt end of the egg), it follows that the egg should be carefully monitored during incubation, and especially so at pipping time. If you are going to use a piece of eggshell for repair, it must first be disinfected. This is best done by placing the pieces of shell in a solution of 20 cc Novassan and one gallon (3.79 L) of water.[3]

Eggshell Damage and Damaged Egg Membrane

The above damages are concerned with the calcified layer and not the egg membrane that lies beneath (there are actually two membranes, but for the sake of practicality, I will treat it here as one). Damage can be such that blood and albumen escape to the exterior of the egg. A slightly torn membrane can be cauterized with a coagulant. I use a cotton swab, slightly moistened in distilled water, and "dip" this in silver nitrate. Be very careful with the cotton swab; don't make the hole even bigger! After the silver nitrate treatment, I finish the repair as described above. As long as the repair is carried out as soon as possible after the damage occurs, there is a good chance that the embryo will continue to develop normally, especially if the vascular system (which you cannot monitor), in spite of the egg membrane damage, continues to function. We must never forget that albumen contains an antibacterial lysozymen to protect the embryo.

After each repair don't forget to put the egg back in the incubator. Remember that the egg may have to have two or three layers of glue and/or gauze, and that each layer must be dry before you apply the next one. If the egg is from a nest box, place it, between repair stages, on a layer of sterile wadding in a box placed in a warm position. Gauze patches must be cut larger than the area of the damage. First place a layer of glue over the area, then cover it with the gauze. As we have already stated, sterile gauze is found in first aid kits and can be purchased from your drugstore. If you have no gauze available, you can use tissue, but gauze is stronger as Jordan says: "It is more three-dimensional than tissue and is more easily removed by moistening it with water and scraping or slicing it off with a razor blade."[4]

Case Report—An Experience in Budgerigar Breeding

I have often explained to others what to do in the case of young birds that had difficulty in hatching. But my knowledge was based on what I had read in books and what other breeders had told me, not from personal experience. In the case of parakeets, I still follow Gerald S. Binks' table to guide my decision whether to assist or stand by (see Table 1, page 8).

If you plan to hand-rear the chick you help to hatch, you can discard the eggshell, but if you want the

---

[3]Rick Jordan, *Parrot Incubation Procedures* (Ontario: Silvio Mattacchione and Co., 1989).
[4]Jordan.

parents to continue to rear the chick, you should put the largest pieces of shell back in the nest. If you don't do this, there is a good chance that the mother will kill the chick! She will "expect" to find an eggshell in the nest, not "suddenly" a moving, begging chick!

Number of Eggs

Whether I allow my birds to breed and rear their young in aviary nest boxes, or remove them for incubation and hand-rearing, it is important to know how many eggs per clutch our birds are likely to lay. There are, naturally, no hard and fast rules, but we do have an idea how many eggs per clutch can be expected from the various species. The low end of the range is held by single-egg laying birds, the Arctic Tern, *Sterna paradisae*, and a species of swallow from Kalimantan, (Indonesian Borneo). The upper end of the range—10 to 20 eggs—is exemplified by the Golden-crowned Kinglet, *Regulus strapa*, which lays up to 10; the Mallard, *Anas platyrhynchos*, which lays up to 16; and the Ring-necked Pheasant, *Phasianus colchicus*, which lays up to 15.

Is that coincidental? No, the number of eggs in the clutches of individual species is important for the species preservation. Birds that lay a single egg select inaccessible places in which to build their nests. The Borneo Swallow, for example, constructs its mud nest at the tip of a very thin, supple twig. Many seabirds lay their eggs on narrow rock ledges, high on cliffs, or rocky islets. Potential predators thus have little chance of finding or gaining access to eggs or chicks.

By comparison, pheasants and ducks often lay their eggs in nests on the open ground—almost an invitation for an egg eater! The general rule we can arrive at is that "the

Table 1
Hatching: Assist or Stand By

Sound	Appearance	Action
Medium squeaks	Cracks and early discoloration	Too soon; replace
Loud squeaks	Crack line around circumference, creamy patches, moist membrane	Normal hatching; replace
Loud squeaks	Crack line around circumference, creamy patches, dried membrane	Assist
Loud squeaks	Large hole, drying membrane	Assist

greater the danger, the larger the number of eggs."

Generally, birds of certain species lay a similar average number of eggs per clutch. The Bobwhite Quail, *Colinus virginianus*, for example lays 7 to 20 eggs; the Herring Gull, *Larus argentatus*, lays 3 to 4; the Long-billed Curlew, *Numenius americanus*, lays 4, sometimes 3 or 5; the Lapwing, *Vanellus vanellus*, lays 4 to 5; and the Ring-necked Duck, *Aythea collaris*, lays 7 to 13, and occasionally more (in the case of very large clutches; however, it may be due to two females using the same nest). A Sharp-shinned Hawk, *Accipiter striatus*, generally lays 5 eggs; a robin, *Turdus migratorius*, 3 to 5; and a house sparrow, *Passer domesticus*, 4 to 6.

In some species there may be a fairly large range of clutch sizes, as in the Ring-necked Duck, and there always seems to be room for expansion. Anyone who has collected lapwing's eggs (an activity that was formerly very popular in Europe but is now illegal in most Western European countries) will know that if you leave one egg in the nest, the female will continue to try and maintain her clutch to its average size for some considerable time, meaning more eggs for the collectors over a period of time. Of course, the record holder for egg laying must be the domestic chicken that had been selectively bred to produce hundreds of eggs a year. The champion must be a White Leghorn hen that reportedly laid 371 eggs in 364 days, ending on August 29, 1979, at the College of Agriculture, University of Missouri.

I once read in a bird magazine about an astonishing clutch of 32 eggs laid by a Zebra Finch. Many years ago, another ornithological magazine, *The Auk*, published an article about the persistent egg-laying marathon of a woodpecker that managed to lay 71 eggs in 73 days! From time to time we continue to hear such amazing reports from pigeon fanciers and aviculturists and no doubt we will continue to do so.

The purpose of this text, however, is not to try for new clutch size records. Pressure to overproduce eggs will tire, stress, and even kill a female bird, while the eggs themselves are likely to become infertile, or the embryos weaker. It is better to aim for good average clutches rather than try and overstress the reproductive powers of your birds!

Nests

The common belief is that all bird species build nests (see Nest Building, page 28), but this is not strictly the case. Many ground-breeding birds, for example, construct no nest at all, or at most a very simple one. Beach birds, like plovers, make do with a small hole twisted out of the sand. Some of them like to decorate the edge of the hollow with a single shell or pebble, probably to help them identify the nest when they come in to land.

Even if a simple hollow in the ground can be considered a nest; it

Canary hen with 7-day-old chicks.

Aegithalos galbula, of Europe, or the various weaverbirds of Africa. Colonies of breeding weavers fill whole acacia trees with their nests, which, viewed from a distance, resemble fruit. In extreme cases, the top of the tree may be covered with a communal roof.

Heights

Nests are built at varying heights from the ground. Lapwings and Horned Larks, *Eremophila alpestri*, build their nests on the ground; the Mockingbird, *Mimus polyglottos*, the Hermit Thrush, *Catharus guttatus*, and various finches build their nests in low shrubs or hedges. The Cooper's Hawk, *Accipiter cooperii*, and the Black-billed Magpie, *Pica pica*, nest high in the trees. Many owls, woodpeckers, and parrots prefer to set up house in hollow limbs, while the Kingfisher, *Megaceryle torquata*, the Sand Martin, *Riparia riparia*, and the Shellduck, *Tadorna tadorna*, nest in excavated burrows in banks at the water's edge.

The elevation of nests can vary quite considerably among some species such as the House Finch, *Carpodactus mexicanus*, and the American Robin, *Turdus migratorius*. Ground cover can be an influence, as with the Swamp Sparrow, *Melospezia georgiana*, which builds in rushes; the Blue-winged Warbler, *Vermivora pinus*, which builds in swamp vegetation; and the Greater Swamp Duck, *Aythea marila nearctica*, and the European Aquatic War-

is certain that brood parasites, like the well-known cuckoo, certainly don't construct one. They lay their eggs in the nest of another species and let the foster parents rear their young. It seems quite strange that cuckoos entrust the care of their young to others, but when we consider that, in nature, everything depends on everything else one way or another, then maybe it isn't so strange after all!

The vast majority of bird species, however, do construct nests of varying complexity. Some of the simplest are those of ground-nesting birds. The lapwing twists a depression in the grass; the quail tries to form the depression into a kind of tunnel. At the other extreme are the attractive and complex nests of birds like the Baltimore Oriole, *Icterus galbula*, of North America, the Long-tailed Tit, bler, *Acrocephalus paludicola*, which build in sedges. Nest elevation can also depend on factors like open topography, as with the Great Gray Shrike, *Lanius excubitor*, or with flowing water, as with several types of swallow.

Human Encroachment

The destruction of natural bird habitats by human encroachment means that birds disappear or at least become extremely rare. A shortage of old hollow trees, for example, has led to the decline of many woodpeckers, Red-breasted Nuthatches, *Sitta canadensis*, tits, and Brown Creepers, *Certhia familiaris*. The logging of old-growth forest in Australia has also led to the demise of many parrots and other hole-nesting species. Similarly, agricultural development has led to the decline of the Hoopoe, *Upupa epops*, the Night Heron, *Nycticorax nycticorax*, and the European Golden Plover, *Pluvialis apricaria*.

Where and When Nests Are Built

Some birds are quite adaptable to change, finding novel substitutes for their natural sites. Nests can be found in mailboxes, old pumps, empty flowerpots, and birdhouses. Birds may even select new construction materials, such as candy wrappers, hair, and wool plucked from clothing.

Observers have discovered that many birds do most of their nest building in the morning, though this differs from species to species. In most cases it is the female that chooses the nest site and does most of the building, but in a number of species, both sexes share in these tasks. As a general rule of thumb, species in which the sexes are more or less identically colored build their nests together, while in species in which there is marked color dimorphism, the female does the nest building but the male may help collecting materials.

Reusing Nests

A question often asked is: "Do birds reuse old nests?" There is no definitive answer to this. We do know that storks and swallows, for example, will return to their same nest year after year, while their offspring also will try to nest in the same vicinity. Some birds, such as the House Finch, the Rock Dove, *Columba livia*, and many crows, like to build their new nests as close as possible to their previous ones. The vast majority of bird species, however, use a nest only once, particularly birds like pheasants, partridges, quail, ducks, and similar species with precocial young. Some species actually construct hiding nests or even trial nests. Good examples of this include the popular Zebra Finch and the Common Wren, in which a single brood may require three or four nests.

In a few cases birds use the same nest for successive broods—the sparrow, the pigeon, and the jackdaw, for example. A popular aviary dove, the Diamond Dove, *Geopelia cuneata*, makes a somewhat untidy nest to begin with but improves it with time. Though never completely attractive to the human eye, the dove's nest does its job.

Brooding Behavior

Birds are mostly seasonal breeders. At the right time of the year, usually triggered by seasonal climatic changes, they come into breeding condition. This means that hormones are released into the bloodstream, making the bird want to court, mate, build a nest, and raise a family. Once the nest is built and the eggs are laid, brooding time has arrived and another change takes place in the bird. People often say, "Birds are broody," or "ready to brood." Old bird lovers used to say, "The birds are running a fever."

Brood Spots

A brooding bird is able to elevate the temperature of certain brood spots on her body and, while sitting on the eggs, she presses these spots against them. Not all birds have their brood spots in the same location; that is why not all birds sit on their eggs in the same way. Take a look at the comfortable, broadly stretched-out domestic hen, which, before settling to brood, arranges her eggs and nest to fit her form pleasurably. Compare this with the super-nervous lapwing, which presses her breast to the eggs and sits with her body steep and pointed, as though she has little time and has urgent business elsewhere. Compare also the deeply settled House Finch with the airy sitting Zebra Finch. Or compare the Robin, which ducks down deep into her nest, with the Cormorant, sitting royally on her throne. These positions are wholly dictated by the location, size, and intensity of the brood spots. Some birds almost seem to sit with their legs tied in knots. The swan usually sticks her legs out behind her, while stilt-legged birds (like curlews and godwits) place theirs far forward. Terns often seem to stand practically over their eggs. Like many people, birds have to struggle with problems well ahead of the time their young arrive. Understandably, birds that don't brood, like our familiar cuckoo, don't have brood spots.

Some species, such as ducks, pluck out the feathers from over their brood spots. While the feathers are used for extra insulation around the nest, the bare brood spots are more efficient in warming the eggs. Strangely, some brooding birds seem to go over the top, ripping out large hanks of feathers from all over their breasts, sometimes resulting in bloody wounds.

Brooding Periods

The time taken to brood a clutch of eggs to hatching varies considerably. There seems to be some correlation with the size of eggs in some cases, but certainly not in all cases. There may be more of a connection with the stage of development at which the chick leaves the egg. There is a range, represented on the low side by well-developed "nest leavers," like chickens and ducks, and on the high side by poorly developed "nest huddlers," like house sparrows and canaries. Let us look at some specific examples.

European and American birds with short brooding periods are represented by the Chaffinch, *Fringilla coelebs*, and the American Robin, *Turdus migratorius*, which take about 13 days to hatch their eggs, with 11 days among the recorded minimums. In midrange among brooders are pheasants (23 to 25 days), the Ring-necked Duck (24 to 27 days), and the American Eider, *Somateria mollissima dresseri*, which takes 26 to 28 days. At the upper end, we have 27 to 30 days for the Kestrel, *Falco tinnunculus*; 28 to 31 days for the Ferruginous Roughleg, *Buteo regalis*; and 33 to 37 days for the Cooper's Hawk, *Accipiter cooperii*.

To say "33 to 37 days for the Cooper's Hawk" means, of course, that in a single clutch, in the same nest, it can take a period of five days between the hatching of the first and the last egg, but generally, for this species, it is hard to state precise statistics because too many factors are involved—temperature (day and night), humidity, wind speed, photoperiod (hours of daylight), and other environmental conditions. Other important facts deal with the individual nature of the brooding bird; things like intensity of brooding,

Black-throated Finches (Poephila cincta) *that are 2 to 3 days old. The nest is generally used for one clutch only, but the material from the first nest is often incorporated into the second one.*

Young cockatiels. When they are about 30 days old they leave the nest, but will continue to be fed by both parents for some time.

26-day-old chick of the silver-eared mesia (Leiothrix argentauris)*. The hen lays 3 or 4 green-blue eggs with red-brown and brown spots and stains. The eggs are practically impossible to distinguish from those of the Pekin Robin.*

frequency of partner switch, tightness of contact with the brood spot, nature and thickness of feathers, nest quality, and tempo with which the eggs are laid, all play their part.

Nest and eggs of the Painted or Chinese Painted Quail (Excalfactoria chinensis)*.*

The notion of this five-day spread is not accepted by everyone because some people do not believe that birds begin to brood until the complete clutch is laid. Most clutches, especially those of small songbirds that lay their eggs at a fast clip (usually one a day), do indeed hatch more or less at the same time. Exceptions do occur, however, in that a small clutch of eggs may take over a day to hatch. Birds that lay larger clutches definitely don't hatch their eggs all at the same time. That is the rule with large predatory species that lay their eggs every *second* day. It is easy for you to confirm this fact, if only by noting the clear difference in size among the nestlings.

Which Partner Broods

Which of the partners does the brooding—male, female, or both (see page 60)? An easy rule of thumb is to look at the coloration of the parents. If they are more or less of the same color, they are likely to take turns brooding. If the female is much plainer in color, she generally broods alone. You never, or almost never, come across a species in which the male has plainer plumage. Plain coloration in the female helps camouflage her in the nest, while the brighter colors of the male serve as a decoy to lead potential predators away from the nest.

Feeding the Female

Does the male feed the brooding female? In most cases, he does. This makes good sense in species where the female is the sole brooder. The male often combines this service with another—guarding the nest and chasing away trespassers. This appealing show of cooperation between the pair is impressive. The falcon exemplifies this: While the female is brooding, the male hunts for food, but he doesn't bring it right to her; she has to come and get it. After killing prey, he brings it near the nest and calls her with his hoarse cries. She joins him, and eats away from the nest to protect her eggs.

Hatchlings

Now a few remarks about new hatchlings (see also pages 34–35). Most young birds break through the shell with the so-called egg tooth, and then break open the shell by pushing with the body. All birds, from sparrows to ostriches, have their heads near the air chamber of the eggs as they incubate, so that all birds leave the egg from more or less the same spot. The adults often eat the remains of the eggshells, but large pieces may be dumped away from the nest, making one less attraction for potential predators.

There are two basic types of hatchling, which I have named "nest leavers" and "nest huddlers," terms that I mentioned in passing when discussing length of brooding (see page 13). Young of the "leavers"—chickens, ducks, pheasants, quail—dry off within a few hours after hatching. Their down is thick enough to protect them consider-

When the young hatch, they look like small, active balls of down.

ably and, after just a few hours, they are trying out their legs and ready to have a look at the world beyond the confines of their mother's feathery shelter. On the second day they are quite ready to join their mother on a

Asking for food. After two weeks the young of the European Blackbird (Turdus merula) leave the cup-shaped nest, which is built with plant matter and lined with mud.

Seven-day-old Black-throated Finches.

habits—present quite a different picture. The new hatchling lies exhausted in the nest, panting, powerless, and blind. Whether it dries off is immaterial, as it is naked, except perhaps for a few sparse patches of down.

Food Requirements

One positive thing the hatchling has is an incredible appetite—its food requirements are enormous! Adult birds also have a relatively substantial appetite. Having a high level of activity and a relatively high body temperature, they require a great deal of food energy to keep them operating efficiently. Young birds, however, eat a great deal more. To develop on schedule and in good health, they can easily eat more than their own body weight in a 24-hour period. The adults, therefore, have to work incredibly hard to keep sufficient food coming in.

food-gathering expedition. They can already pick up morsels of food on their own and the adult care principally involves leading the young to food and providing refuge beneath protective wings.

The "nest huddlers"—canaries, house sparrows, and birds of similar

Ornithologists who like statistics have counted feeding flights repeatedly for a number of species. These counts require observation from sunrise to sunset because the trips to food source and back differ in length. The observer must record actual flights, not just project an average from a few samples. I have done this work myself and became convinced that the statistics recorded by others are not exaggerated.

Dr. A. A. Allen, a highly respected professor of ornithology at Cornell University, made a motion picture of a female wren who made 1,217 food-bearing flights between a single

One-month-old Plum-headed Finches (Aidemosyne molesta). *They like a well-planted long flight to "grow up" in.*

This Green-winged Macaw (Ara chloroptera) was hand-raised by the author. This species usually proves to be a reliable breeder.

The budgerigar or parakeet is by far the most popular pet bird in the world—and rightly so!

sunrise and sunset. Dr. J. P. Thyssen, a Dutch ornithologist, scored an even higher record for a Black-capped Chickadee, with an amazing 1,356 trips.

Feeding the Hatchlings

Is this largesse shared fairly among the young? If so, how? Nature helps parent birds wondrously in this potentially tricky task (see also page 63). All the adult has to do is pop the feed it's carrying into any random open bill; a helpful reflex takes care of proper distribution. The system works as follows: When food reaches the throat of a young bird, a swallowing reflex is triggered. This works more promptly and more actively when the crop is emptier. Conversely, when the crop is fuller, the swallowing reflex is slower; therefore, once a parent bird drops a morsel into an open beak, the adult watches what happens. If the food doesn't get swallowed fast enough, the adult deftly removes the morsel and gives it to another of the young. Only the chick that swallows promptly and quickly gets to keep the food.

Droppings

In addition to carrying the food in, the adult has to carry the young birds' droppings out. After bringing in a beakful of food and watching it disappear, the adult pauses watchfully for a moment, observing the previously fed young. When one rises to deposit a dropping on the edge of the nest, the parent bird snatches up the dropping. Droppings are conveniently packaged by nature inside a membrane, making them easy to pick up and drop off away from the nest. Most birds do this. It keeps the nest clean and keeps enemies away who would be attracted by the smell. However, some droppings can still be found on and near the nest whenever foraging trips take too long. The digestive process then is too fast for the adults to keep up with.

Leaving the Nest

In most small bird species, the young leave the nest only 8 to 14 days after hatching. Generally speaking, the bigger the bird species, the longer it takes them to fledge.

Feathers

On hatching, the young are covered with down, not feathers. These develop between the down a little later, first appearing as closed, rolled-up "stubble." The "flag" of the feather starts to appear when the stubble is about a quarter of its length.

Size of Young Birds

Have you ever noticed that a young bird is bigger and heavier than an adult one? It is generally supposed that an animal always progresses toward greater height and weight as it grows to adulthood, but that's not true for birds.

A young bird on its maiden flight can be 25 percent heavier than an adult; it has just passed through an inactive stage with an excellent supply of food. A far more active stage now begins, with less food available and more effort required to secure it. The extra body weight helps tide the youngster over this difficult time. A bird hatched in spring reaches its "normal" adult weight only in October or November.

That's pretty much our story about nests, eggs, and young—but the story isn't static. Look around for yourself in nature and in your aviary. You will often discover something special. In 1982, not far from my home in The Netherlands, we found a Redstart nest with a cuckoo's egg in it (the Redstart, *Phoenicurus phoenicurus*, is named not for its takeoff, but for its tail—"staart" in Dutch). We also discovered a nest of Spotted Flycatchers, *Muscipapa striata*, that had the interior lined with toffee wrappers. And we found the nest of a Chaffinch, *Fringilla coelebs*, that was lined with threads from coats and shawls. Take an opportunity for an outing and enjoy the novelties of nature whenever possible.

Inside the Eggshell

At the beginning of this chapter we discussed the eggshell in detail because, as bird breeders, we must have good knowledge of the subject. We also know that *inside* the shell a new life is developing. The egg is truly a wonderful thing! It possesses everything that is necessary for the development of an embryo. After a certain incubation period, a chick hatches; in the case of the "nest leavers" (precocial or nidifugous birds), the hatchling is well developed, with open eyes, a thick downy coat, and able to walk and leave the nest. In the case of the "nest huddlers" (altricial or nidicolous birds), the hatchling is quite helpless.

The Ovaries and Oviduct

How does the egg develop in the maternal body? The ovaries are located in the posterior part of the female body cavity. They are suspended from the back by a special ligament and appear to be unbalanced, due to the fact that in most species of birds, only the left ovary develops while the right remains vestigeal or is even absent. Of course, there are exceptions: in some raptors, the right ovary is normally developed, and that is the case with many other birds. Examination of 200 adult female Wood Pigeons, *Columba palumbas*, showed that 23.5 percent had a developed right ovary; in 22 female house sparrows that were examined, 4.5 percent. It is therefore not a rarity for a bird species to have a functional right ovary.

If only the left ovary is developed in a female bird, there is also only a single oviduct—the left, while the right oviduct is totally absent.

Breeding Season

During the breeding season—in the spring for most species—the ovarian follicles begin to grow in size in the lining of the ovary. As

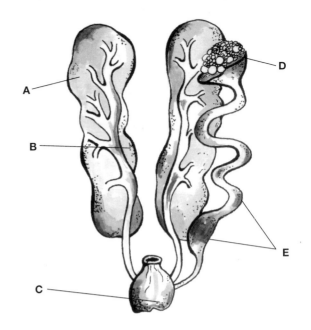

The Female Reproductive System
A. Kidney
B. Ureter
C. Cloaca
D. Ovary
E. Oviduct

you probably know, in the world of plants and animals, nature has invented unique mechanisms to ensure the maintenance of the various species—in our discussion, species of birds. I will give you an example: In the ovaries of young Jackdaws, *Corvus monedula,* 24,500 to 26,000 follicles have been counted; these have a diameter of 39 to 50μ (μ = 1/1000 mm). At the beginning of the breeding season, a number of these generally begin to ripen. In Jackdaws the number is 18 to 37. The eventual clutch of a Jackdaw, which only breeds for a few years, is four to six, occasionally two to nine eggs. Here, nature has also taken care: If, for one reason or another, the first clutch is lost, then a second, or even a third clutch can be produced in a short

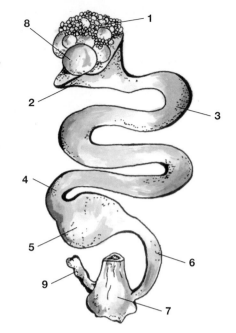

*Female Repro-
ductive System
(Close-up)*
1. *Ovary*
2. *Infundibulum*
3. *Magnum*
4. *Isthmus*
5. *Uterus (Shell
   gland)*
6. *Vagina*
7. *Cloaca*
8. *Mature ovum*
9. *Redundant
   ovary*

time. A similar phenomenon can be seen, for example, in many Australian finches and parrots: If conditions are bad (as in a drought, when seed and other foods are scarce), they don't or hardly breed; however, as soon as the table is laid, which means, as soon as the rains come and food becomes plentiful, these birds can hastily raise two or more broods before conditions again become harsh.

As the yolk develops, the eggs become slowly macroscopic, and thus visible to the naked eye. But they are still only egg cells, which means they consist only of one cell. We have a case here of being able to see a single cell without the use of a microscope. Cells are, in other cases, the smallest building blocks in the tis-

sues of plants and animals and are not usually visible to the naked eye.

At the beginning of the breeding season, the ovary visibly increases in size. It has the appearance of a small bunch of grapes, due to the mass of little egg cells. With the build-up of the yolk, these little "bubbles," or follicles, act as small vessels, attached to the ovary walls by narrow stems. All follicles are surrounded by a layer of ovary cells. The largest hang freely in the body cavity. As soon as an ovum is released from the follicle and taken up by the oviduct, the follicle resembles a limp sack that quickly shrivels away and, in the Jackdaw, in 8 to 12 days, is no longer visible. When a clutch of eggs has been laid, the remaining follicles quickly degenerate and, again in the Jackdaw, for example, the ovary returns to its original form in two to three weeks.

Following the Egg on Its Way

Now let us follow the egg on its way. When the follicle bursts, it releases the egg from the ovary. The egg enters the funnellike opening of the oviduct. This is a thin, walled tube that is held in the correct position by elastic ligaments situated just behind the ovary, so that, when a ripe egg breaks loose from the ovary, it is taken up by the "funnel" of the oviduct.

The oviduct itself is a muscular, coiled tube lined with a mucous membrane, which releases albumin from certain glands. At the beginning of the breeding season, the oviduct increases both in size and width. Fertilization of the egg takes place in the upper part of the oviduct, before the release of albumin and the formation of the membranes and the shell.

A single act of copulation can be adequate to fertilize all of the eggs in a clutch, but most birds copulate regularly—before laying begins, during laying, and even during brooding.

Cleavage

Once fertilized, the egg cell begins to divide (*cleavage*) at the *blastodisk*, which lies on the surface of the yolk, the start of the development of the embryo. This cleavage process occurs on a relatively small area of the egg that, in birds, is known as *diskoidal cleavage*. The large yolk mass is not affected. The eggs of birds (and reptiles) are remarkable for the size of their yolks. This yolk, which is contained in a membrane, forms, together with the blastodisk, the egg. The yolk of a bird's egg is composed of two layers, the white, and the yellow yolk, which differ in color and makeup. If you cut through a hard-boiled chicken's egg, you can see the two sorts of yolk, arranged concentrically.

The white yolk forms the outer layer and curves in a little at the spot where the blastodisk is situated, forming a compact nucleus. The ratio of the weight of the yolk to that of the egg is not always the same. With well-developed nest leavers, the yolk

weight is about one third more (to 40 percent) while that of nest huddlers is only 18 to 20 percent of the weight of the freshly laid egg.

Chalazen

Let us return to the oviduct. As the ovum travels along the duct, it is layered with thick albumen, the outer layers consisting of thinner fluidy albumen. Two twisted, cord-like structures called *chalazen* are formed by part of the dense albumen. These suspend the yolk in the mass of albumen from the poles of the egg. When the egg is turned, the yolk always rights itself with the vegetative part below, the animal part above. Scientists believe that in this manner the embryo can always receive maximum warmth from a brooding parent. The chalazen also act as shock absorbers in case of bumps and vibrations.

Egg Membrane

In the center of the oviduct the next process begins. The albumen, which now totally encloses the yolk, is covered with a membrane that is formed from certain substances released by glands. This shell membrane consists also of two close layers, as we have already seen (see page 7), which, at the thick end of the egg, separate to form an air sac. The presence of the membrane is easy to see when you peel a boiled hen's egg. If you don't immediately put the freshly boiled egg into cold water, the membrane will stick to the firm albumen, making the egg more difficult to peel than if it stuck to the inside of the shell.

The Uterus

The third part of the oviduct is the uterus, where the egg receives its hard outer shell, as we have discussed in the earlier part of this chapter (see page 2).

The Vagina

The fourth and last part of the oviduct is the vagina, a muscular tube that opens into the cloaca. Glands in the walls of the vagina secrete ample mucus that helps release the egg at laying time.

To summarize, we can say that the egg is a living cell, protected by a number of defensive layers (hard, calcified shell, double shell membrane, and a thick layer of antibacterial albumen). The egg is alive, it breathes, and therefore we must treat it with respect if we want a healthy, lively chick to hatch from it!

Chapter Two
Natural Incubation

Making the Most of Your Hobby

Although this book is concerned with artificial incubation—that is, hatching eggs in an incubator and hand-rearing pet birds—many aviculturists allow the birds to do the job themselves. It is also nice to let birds that normally "work for the incubator" have the occasional shot at brooding and raising themselves. We will return to this later (see page 28). Let us first make a few comments on the natural breeding of pet birds.

Successful natural hatchings require a calm, stable environment. Don't start breeding in cages and aviaries too early in the year. In general, the safest period is from the end of April or early May until mid-September. In most cases, birds (like parakeets, cockatiels, finches, and canaries) will breed two to three times per season. More frequent breeding should be discouraged, to avoid risking losses from egg binding (see page 141) and such.

As soon as the chicks (like lovebirds, parakeets, conures, Australian hookbills, finches, and canaries) are independent, they ordinarily should be kept apart from the parents and placed in a separate roomy cage or aviary; otherwise, further breeding by the parents is inhibited. In addition to seed and/or pellets, egg food (universal), fruits, and greens, supply oystergrit and cuttlebone. Don't give charcoal (there are grit mixes that contain charcoal pieces) as it is suspected of absorbing vitamins A, B_2, and K from the intestinal tract. If this is correct, it can mean that charcoal can cause vitamin deficiency diseases. Grit, by the way, also frequently contains crushed quartz,

Cuttlebone supplies essential minerals to all birds. The wire holder can be made or purchased.

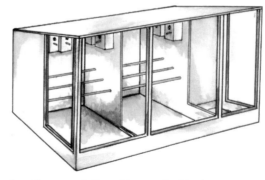

An aviary consisting of two parts; ideal for breeding Australian grass parakeets, budgerigars (parakeets), cockatiels, and lovebirds. The safety porch on the right will ensure that the birds cannot escape from the aviary.

There are many nest box designs that are acceptable as nesting sides to a wide number of bird species.

Even raising a family in the snow is possible! The Red-fronted Macaw (Ara rubrogenys) shows an interesting variation from most other macaw species, in the almost total absence of the typical, bare cheek patch. In this species the patch is limited to a small area just below the eye.

which is very hard, insoluble, and has sharp edges that give a better grinding effect in the gizzard. Nevertheless, in the wild, various birds (Gouldians, for example) take little bits of charcoal before going to nest, but the necessity of a daily supply of charcoal is questionable. Furthermore, adding several drops of a vita-min/mineral preparation to water or seed (I like to give vitamin/mineral drops, instead of powder, through commercial, soft egg food [CéDé, for example], or sprinkled on greens—spinach, lettuce, endive, fresh corn, tomatoes, carrot tops, dandelion, watercress, milk thistle, chickweed, and foxtail, for example—or brown bread) can be advantageous, but don't overdo it, as too great a dose can be dangerous to birds. Don't use cod-liver oil too often as it quickly loses its potency in strong light, and also becomes rancid. If you use cod-liver oil, give,

Outdoor aviary for a mixed bird collection.

at the most, two or three drops for every two pounds (0.76 kg) of seed or quart (0.95 L) of water.

Many hobbyists believe that seed-eating birds also raise their young exclusively on seed. That certainly isn't so! Most bird species feed insects. So, at breeding time, make available a steady supply of ant pupae ("ants eggs"), enchytrae or whiteworms, maggots, small mealworms (cut-up), grasshoppers, small beetles, spiders, earwigs, greenflies, mosquito larvae, water-fleas (*Daphnia*), tubifex, and the like. Also provide old wholemeal or "brown" (NO white) bread, soaked in water and honey, twice a week, as much as the birds can use in a couple of hours.

Selecting and Managing Breeding Stock

Select small birds (finches, canaries, parakeets, lovebirds, etc.) for breeding that are not too old or too young (minimum 12 to 16 months). That's important. For big-ger birds, look up specific refer-ences giving the best time for breeding. Small exotics should be, as stated, at least 12 months old, although there are species in which the minimum age is eight months. If allowed to breed when they are too young, female birds tend to become egg bound far too often, or they don't raise their young properly.

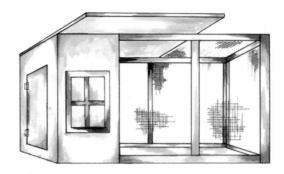

An aviary consisting of three parts: a night shelter (left), a half-open section (with the top covered by a sheet of corrugated fiberglass or similar material), and an open area (right), called the "flight" or "run."

Smaller birds (like most finches, for example) over four or five years of age are unsuitable for breeding. The larger hookbills are not ready to breed before the second, third, or even sixth years. Ordinarily, older males become sterile, or egg laying becomes difficult for the female, which also can cause egg binding.

Depending on their geographic location, many cage and aviary

Outdoor aviary for parakeets or parrots.

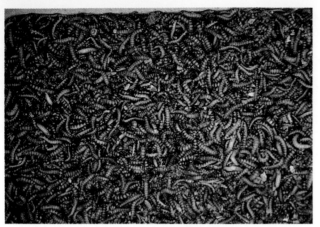

Buffalo worms and other similar worms should be available to your soft-billed birds throughout the year and during the breeding season for many seed-eating birds.

birds have to be deliberately held back from breeding too early. Left to their own devices, they'd already be sitting on eggs in the heart of the winter and would hatch young in the barren season. This early breeding often drains the females, something that can cause unpleasant results in later hatchings. The young from the early hatchings generally are weak, which comes to the fore especially when they, in turn, are ready to be bred. The breeder also should refrain from using sunlamps and other artificial gadgets to extend the breeding season.

When to Breed

Until the proper breeding season starts, keep breeding pairs separated—males with males, and females with females. If you put on

the correct leg bands (see page 54), sexing is easy.

If your birds start breeding at the end of April or early May, you can expect two or three clutches from most species. You will be able to distinguish birds hatched this way by their pure color and their healthy appearance, provided, of course, they were properly housed and fed.

Be guided by the weather about the time to start breeding. Bad weather can ruin a hatch in outdoor aviaries—certainly in places where wet, chilly weather is normal in early spring. You may miss a potential hatch by waiting out the bad weather but that is more than offset by the fact that the young you do hatch stand out in quality and good health, and that your breeders stay healthy and strong, ready for successful breeding in the next season. Conversely, if you breed too early, the young tend to come out weak, don't feather out well, and could become fatally ill from just a few days of exposure to bad weather. And the breeders themselves tend to get sick and strained from overwork.

I cannot overemphasize that breeding pairs must be disease-free. Believe me—healthy young can be raised only out of totally healthy parents.

Pairing Off

When breeding several birds, separate the pairs from each other before the breeding season. I use small exhibition cages in which I isolate selected pairs for about two weeks. I don't provide any nesting material in these cages, nor do I attach nest boxes. The birds simply sit and eat, as well they should, because a reserve layer of fat put on now will stand them in good stead later. The purpose of this isolation is to get birds used to each other, to promote *pair bonding*. Pairs bonded in this way almost always stay together the entire breeding season after they are released into the aviary or colony breeding cage. I can check on whether my selected matings work by keeping track of individuals by their color-coded leg bands (see page 54).

When several pairs of the same species are housed together, they should be *homozygous* (purebred) for color. This precaution prevents problems when pairs put together by the breeder don't stay together, once they come into contact with other birds of the same species. Birds, like people, prefer to select their own mates.

It may happen that two birds you have selected as mates don't make it as a pair. You see evidence of this when a pair keeps starting and restarting its nest building, or the female may lay abnormally large clutches of eggs that the birds then cover up by a new nest several days later. I've noticed this especially in Zebra Finches.

The best response is to separate these unsuccessful couples and remate them with other birds. In most cases, this solution seems to cure troubles of this sort.

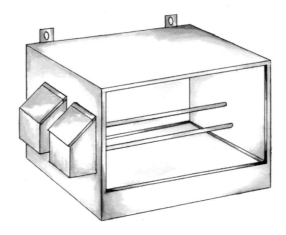

Breeding cage. There are many different sizes and types of box cages available, but when the birds are to be bred, many aviculturists prefer this cage to all other types!

Many aviary birds like to nest in a breeding box. Attach these boxes at varying heights, but not too low. Keep them away from perches and resting places to prevent the birds from soiling one another. Also, keep the boxes away from food and water containers.

Wooden nest boxes for canaries and finches.

Breeding cages for Australian grass finches and waxbills.

Nest Building

Tropical and subtropical birds are generally industrious, enthusiastically raising brood after brood. The tendency is particularly strong in domesticated birds like budgerigars, lovebirds, cockatiels, canaries, Bengalese, Cutthroat Finches, and Zebra Finches. This shows especially in nest-building birds, such as Zebra Finches, in their building activities. The male Zebra Finches do most of the work; they'll snatch up the nesting material as soon as you give it to them, and begin looking for a proper construction site with a big piece of building material already in their beaks.

The male nervously goes about the site selection, while the female tends to stay calmer. She seems more concerned about her important task to follow, often limiting herself to ordering and arranging the nesting material brought in by her mate. However, there are exceptions. I have had females in my aviary that got involved with carrying material to the nest under construction. In other cases I have seen a female that selected nesting material and placed her selections in the beak of her mate, for him to carry to the nest site. I like to observe my birds working together.

A few birds, however, may be rather slow in starting nest construction. There isn't much you can do about this, other than allow the other birds in the aviary to set the pace. In most cases, slow nesters

Author's breeding room for budgerigars (parakeets).

will soon get the idea after seeing the industry of the other birds.

Nesting Material

Be selective in the types of nesting material you give your birds. Dry hay and sisal rope strands are recommended as basic materials, but if birds need other items, such as moss or twigs, look for specific needs of the different species in books dealing with various cage and aviary bird species (see Useful Literature and Addresses, page 143). The two basic nest materials let the birds build neatly, and come up with strong, safe nests.

Breeding cages for lovebirds, **Forpus** *species, and parakeets.*

Be sure to separate the rope strands and cut them into short pieces. I think pieces about 2½ inches (6 cm) long are about right. Longer pieces seem to be difficult for the birds to handle in nest construction. They're also unwieldy for the birds to carry through the aviary, and tend to get entangled in their legs. Birds can get into serious

Cockatiels kept in cages and aviaries are often more comfortable with natural nest boxes and natural perches. From her vantage point, this normal (-wild) colored hen surveys her domain.

Author's breeding cages for lovebirds.

Colony breeding **(Peach-faced Lovebirds).**

trouble this way, and could be killed unless quickly rescued. The problem often occurs in quail and similar birds, particularly in those species that have a strong growth of nails.

Provide dry hay alone at first, then add rope strands later. The timing may be difficult in aviaries where several couples are nesting, but use

Modern breeding facilities. Note the skylight.

your own judgment and do your best to have breeding pairs kept close to the same schedule. If breeding is not synchronized, however, don't be overly worried. If you show the birds clearly that building materials of two different types are furnished in separate racks, they usually will first use the hay to build the bowl of the nest, and then the rope for the balance of the construction.

Most species build rather coarse nests, but some build distinctively artistic ones. In most cases, aviary birds use hay for the outside construction. The inside is then carefully lined with rope strands, horsehair, wool, feathers, and anything else that might be available.

There are no absolute rules about nesting materials, although I counsel against randomly supplying anything at hand. Wool, strips of toilet paper, hair, yarn, and bits of textile material are all accepted. Small exotics, such as waxbills and Australian grass finches, like carpet wool, and they also welcome pieces of hemp rope. Natural colors are best for nesting materials. Birds will accept red, blue, or green material, but with less enthusiasm.

It's a good practice to provide only enough material the birds will require for one round of nest building. Some birds, Zebra Finches, in particular, can get carried away with the job. They keep on building until there is not a shred of nesting material left in the aviary and, even though the female may do only the "interior decorating," she can get

Nest box occupied by a family of Black-throated Finches. Almost any type of nesting material will be utilized for nest building, but preference will be given to long lengths of coarse grass for the actual nest, soft grass for the inside, and feathers for the lining.

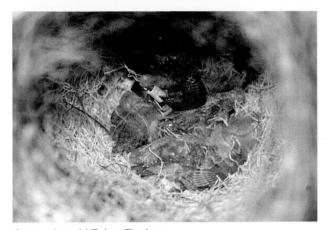

Seven-day-old Zebra Finches.

so absorbed in this work that she forgets about laying eggs!

When the nest is arranged to the birds' satisfaction—after three or four days of work—the female Zebra Finch is ready for the amorous attentions of her mate. She starts beating her tail up and down and from right to left as a sign she is ready to mate. The order of business—first nest building, then copulation—isn't absolute. Some birds mate first, then build a nest (see also page 12).

Inspecting Nests

You may want to check on how the egg laying is progressing, but don't overdo it. Don't worry if the egg count doesn't match the clutch size you read about in textbooks; later clutches may be larger.

The reason nest inspections can be risky is that some birds react strongly to being disturbed while brooding. They may even abandon the nest. Most birds, fortunately, are not that way. I remember having

Nest box occupied by a family of Plum-headed Finches. This species is known for its closely woven nest made of soft grass and completely lined with small feathers.

Birds of varying species need nest boxes of varying design. The nest box shown here will suit virtually any small cage and aviary bird; for example: all Australian grass finches, Mannikins, all small African finches (waxbills), Pekin Robin, and lovebirds.

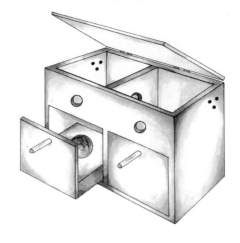

A double nest box with a "pull-out" drawer, often used for breeding para- keets (budgies), allows eggs and nestlings to be observed with minimum disturbance.

This nest box (7.9 inches [20 cm] × 7.9 inches [20 cm] × 23.6 inches [60 cm], with an entrance that is 3.2 inches [8 cm] in diameter) can be used for various medium-sized parrots. Attach a mesh "ladder" to the inner surface, enabling the birds to move out easily.

to move an entire nest full of Zebra Finch eggs from one aviary to another. The parents took to the move calmly, continued brooding as before, and raised a first-rate brood of young.

You can check for unfertilized eggs by lifting them out of the nest with a plastic spoon. Don't use your fingers because the thin eggshell is easy to damage. The smallest crack can potentially be fatal if untreated. Cracks, however, can be fixed (see Eggshell Repair, pages 6–8).

When I check for unfertilized eggs, I do so after the female has been brooding for eight days. Even that check is not always necessary, as birds often discard unfertilized eggs on their own, either by pushing them out of the nest or onto the edge of it.

Candling

Candling, or holding an egg in front of a strong light is the best way to test it for fertility. I have constructed a candling box with a compartment for the egg on top and a socket for a 40 watt bulb below. The egg compartment has a floor made of narrow-mesh woolen netting. I've seen ordinary hairnets used successfully in the same way. The important thing is to have a net soft enough to prevent cracking and a mesh narrow enough to keep the eggs from falling through. There are also some excellent egg candlers available on the market (see pages 144–145).

A cursory look can distinguish fertilized eggs from unfertilized eggs; the lamp light will show you the embryo in the fertile ones. You

Baby canaries ready to be hand-fed.

can see movement—the beginning of life—but don't get carried away by watching the miracle of life because the intense heat of the light bulb isn't good for the embryo; too much exposure would kill it.

Candling of an egg.

Two-week-old Forpus *species.*

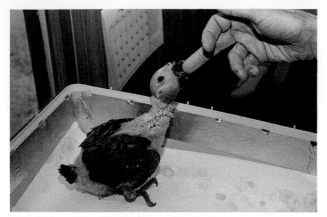

This African Gray Parrot seems hungry!

And don't candle the egg more than once.

If you wait longer than 8 to 12 days (depending on the species), you don't need a candler to check eggs. You don't even have to pick them up. Infertile eggs look pale red ("dirty red," some people say). Fertilized eggs, in contrast, can be distinguished starting about five days after onset of brooding, by their purplish brown, shiny tint.

After Hatching

After waiting, patiently or impatiently, for your hatchlings, they have arrived. What do you do next? Interfere as little as possible. The parents know their task. They have preserved their natural instincts and follow them in the aviary as much as in nature. Therefore, control your enthusiasm. When feeding and watering, let your movements be calm. If you show your hatchlings to visitors, have everyone talk quietly

and without gestures. Keep visitors well away from the edge of the aviary. No matter how quiet visitors are, the birds get nervous just from having people around.

If all goes well, you'll soon see the hatchlings being stuffed full of food the parents have predigested in their crops. You'll see bits and pieces of the eggshells being eaten by the adult birds, while the larger shards are carried off or worked into the nest wall.

Depending on the species, you'll be able to hear the begging cry of the hatchlings after about a week. You may also notice the fluorescent spots (papillae) on the beaks and tips of the tongues of many hatchlings (for example, Australian grass finches). They differ somewhat in

This beer barrel for various large macaws and cockatoos should be reinforced around the entrance to protect the edge of the wood.

color and light intensity (depending on the species), serving as a feeding guide and stimulant to the food-gathering parents.

Be aware that mishaps can occur in the aviary, as in the wild. One of the adult birds, on its way out of the nest, may get its leg entangled in one of the young and drag it away. The young bird falls to the floor, but if you pick it up quickly, and replace it in the nest gently, it will probably recover surprisingly fast. You can reduce such accidents by disturbing the nest as little as possible. In some cases, it may be necessary for you to hand-rear an abandoned nestling—and this book will tell you how (see page 102)!

Twenty-one-day-old **Forpus-*species*.**

Almost Grown

If an older nestling flutters out of the nest a few days early, don't pick it up without thinking first. It may be oppressively hot in the crowded nest, where four or more husky youngsters may be jostling each other for space. If it is warm enough in the aviary, let the enterprising would-be fledgling spend a few days on the aviary floor. It will get the food it needs.

If the young bird is still small and poorly feathered, or if you expect rain or high winds, it is best to put the escapee back in its nest. Hold it in your hand in front of the nest opening and wait quietly until the birds inside calm down completely. Then put the bird back with its brothers and sisters. It is quite pos-

sible that the same bird will leave home again the next day, often early in the morning. Then, just let it be. These precocious nest leavers are disquieting and tend to stimulate the rest of the brood to leave home too. You don't need that! The basic rule

Thirty-three-day-old parakeets.

This Horned Parakeet (Eunymphicus cornutus uvaeensis), raised by the author, is an interesting species. It has a crest similar to that of a cockatiel, but the crest is without erectable power.

attention, the begging young start screaming for food louder and more piercingly until it's often possible to hear them from several dozen yards away. After about two weeks, most young birds can pretty well find their own food, but even so, they still like to beg for it.

The older hatchlings don't confine their begging to their own parents but extend it to other birds trying to feed their young. The strange thing is that practically the whole aviary population helps raise the beggars and makes them independent. Once hatchlings reach independence, you must keep them from breeding. Starting into egg production would be harmful, because the young females are not yet fully developed internally. Their immaturity is reflected on the outside also, since they lack adult coloration. So, remove the young birds, identify them individually and by sex with colored leg bands (see page 54), and isolate the males from the females in separate cages.

Small birds like finches, parakeets, lovebirds, and quail can be considered fully sexually mature when they're 12 to 16 months old, although larger species take obviously longer, sometimes 5 to 7 years as in cockatoos. They can be used for breeding after that.

Closing the Breeding Season

With most birds, natural breeding ought to stop completely by

is, it's okay for young birds to leave the nest when they're fully feathered; otherwise, you have to help!

Some birds at that stage are still more than pleased to keep accepting free meals from Mom and Dad. I enjoy seeing young Zebra Finches beg for food. They beat their wings passionately, almost dragging them along the floor, and they turn their heads in the strangest ways. If Mom and Dad don't pay immediate

September 1. Yes, one could start a new brood in September, but before the young birds are raised and independent, you're into October and November, generally not a favorable time for them. They turn out to be delicate, less attractive, and poor breeders for the next season. They also tend to lay infertile eggs and abandon their nests—just to name a few problems.

Your energy is better directed at giving the aviary a fall cleanup and to taking a good inventory. Furthermore, and more important, the birds will benefit from the nice, long rest; after all, they often literally worked their tails off during the breeding season. Next year, they'll have to raise another couple or three broods. So, separate your breeding pairs and let them relax.

If you want to, you can cage a canary, Pekin Robin (*Leiothrix lutea*), Green Singing Finch (*Serinus mozambicus*), budgerigar, various parrot species, or mynah bird by itself if it is intended as a pet. The bird won't lose luster as long as it has human company every day. Most other birds need to be kept as pairs, but it really depends on the species. In most cases, three pairs of the same species together in an aviary are fine—but two pairs are definitely not recommended.

Chapter Three
The Nursery

Introduction

It is a well-known fact that the artificial incubation of, for example, gallinacious birds (pheasants, quail), waterfowl (ducks, geese), and even large ratites (Rheiformes), all of which are precocial (nest leavers), has taken place on a large scale, without many difficulties, over many years. The young can usually be hand-reared, without the help of the birds' parents. Of course, there are exceptions; the young of the common crane, for example, form such a close bond with their human foster parent that, unless special precautions are taken, they will be quite useless for breeding when they mature.

Today, with the help of modern, sophisticated incubators, we can hatch the eggs of altricial (nest huddlers) birds. At the present time, with an eye to conservation (and rightly so!) the eggs of large parrots and parakeets are being artificially incubated and successfully hatched, and the young hand-raised with commercial rearing foods. The eggs of smaller bird species, such as finches, are usually first incubated and hatched by their own parents, or by foster parents, and then raised by hand, although this requires much patience and know-how (see page 126).

Eggs abandoned by the adult birds, for one reason or another, can be placed with foster parents; for example, chabos can be used for the eggs of small quail species, the domesticated form of the Muscovy Duck for many species of waterfowl, Society Finches (Bengalese) for many small seed-eating birds, especially finches, and the Bourke's Parakeet or Red-rumped Parakeet (to name just two) for many species of parakeet.

There are various reasons why one would want to incubate eggs artificially, such as the following:
- when breeding pairs that, for one reason or another, fail to brood properly;
- when one of a breeding partner dies. If it is the hen—the one that, in most cases, incubates the eggs—the eggs can be divided up among nests of the same species, or with foster parents (try to synchronize hatching times, which is especially important with "group birds," such as parakeets, lovebirds, cockatiels, and similar birds). If this is not a

Table 2
Normal and Maximum Number of Eggs per Annum

Bird Species	Normal Number of Eggs per Clutch	Maximum Number of Eggs per Annum
Canary	4 to 6	60
Dove	2	50
Duck	5 to 14	146
English House Sparrow	4 to 6	60
Goose	10 to 15	100
Guinea Fowl	14	100
Indian Peafowl	5 to 9	37
Ostrich	12 to 15	160
Pheasant	10 to 12	104
Turkey	15 to 20	205
Zebra Finch	4 to 5	72

possibility, the incubator is the only answer to avoid losing the eggs;

- when eggs are laid outside the normal breeding season when natural brooding and rearing success would be at a minimum;
- when the hobbyist wants to raise more than the usual number of broods, especially those of expensive or rare birds.

By regularly removing eggs from a nest immediately after they are laid (and not replacing them with artificial eggs), we can persuade some birds to lay more than the usual number of eggs in the clutch. In a way, we are tricking the hen into thinking its clutch is incomplete, causing it to keep trying to bring up the numbers of eggs (see also page 8). Experiments by various aviculturists have produced some interesting results. In the Japanese Quail (*Coturnix c. japonica*), for example, certain hens have pro-duced more than 360 eggs in a single year—with a record of 364! You must remember, of course, that in the wild this species raises only two clutches of 10 to 15 eggs per season, thus, a maximum of 30 eggs per season. Commercial Japanese Quail hens lay an average of 250 eggs per annum—a surprisingly large number!

The table shown above paints a fascinating picture, though I hope nobody tries it out, for obvious reasons!

Setting up and Equipping the Nursery

With artificial incubation we try to get conditions as close to natural as possible. The most important factors are the correct temperature, relative humidity, ventilation, and

Society Finches or Bengalese have an excellent reputation as foster parents.

regular turning of the eggs. Experience has shown that birds incubated and raised in a well-equipped nursery that is operated by a knowledgeable and skillful aviculturist are less likely to have feeding problems and diseases than those raised by their natural parents or foster parents.

Today many birds are thus brought into the world with the help of an incubator, often located in a special room in the house. Such rooms frequently have a filtered ventilation system, so that the air is kept as free as possible from potentially dangerous bacteria and other organisms. Good hygienic practices must be conducted if we are to keep potentially fatal diseases out of our stock.

Of course, not all aviculturists have an entire special room available to use as a nursery. Many hobbyists initially have to make do with a corner of a room, den, or kitchen, where they can put their incubator, per-

haps sharing space with a microwave oven and some kind of a filtration system. After each season, the bird breeder's "wish list" gets ever longer, until eventually he or she completely takes over an entire room as a nursery.

The Incubator

The incubator is the most important "instrument," and a fascinating instrument it is! As I have already said, the use of incubators, especially for nest leavers, is not a new innovation. Thousands of years ago, the ancient Egyptians and Chinese had already developed a means of artificially incubating the eggs of, primarily, domestic fowl (see page 65). The Egyptians built large compartmented incubation sheds. A fire was maintained in each of the compartments, which were interconnected with manholes. The "chicken brooder" tested the temperature of the eggs by holding them against his eye, then moving them closer to, or further away from the fire as necessary. The Chinese burned charcoal for warming the eggs, but also knew another system whereby fermenting manure was used, the warmth being just enough to incubate the eggs.

At the end of the nineteenth century, incubators were developed and, over the years, these have been progressively refined and automated. The use of electrical power led to great improvement in incubators. The poultry industry uses fully automated machines with a capacity for thousands of eggs.

Necessary Supplies

Hobbyists and aviculturists should best start with a small incubator; there are several excellent makes on the market (see page 144). The simplest are known as still-air incubators (see page 72), and I recommend these for the beginner. The model you choose will depend on the amount of available space you have. Install your incubator in an area where temperature and humidity can be maintained as constantly as possible. Ventilation is also important, but cold drafts are to be avoided at all costs. If the room is too warm, there will be little air circulation in the still-air incubator, perhaps causing the hygrometer to give a false reading. You will understand, of course, that even a short period of overheating can be fatal to your valuable eggs. Even if you only use a corner of a room, den, or kitchen, you must try to take these points into consideration.

The still-air incubator should be placed on a solid, level *table* with a *multi-outlet electrical socket* close by. The table should have as large a surface as possible, as you will need to place several more utensils on it. An alternative is to use two or more tables placed next to each other to make a long bench. All the tables should preferably be the same size and all should be covered with thick plastic, so that the surfaces can be easily cleaned and disinfected when necessary, for example after feeding a clutch of chicks. Hygiene is an extremely important factor; it should *not* be regarded nonchalantly.

Wherever you set up your nursery, it is important (as we have already stated) to install a good filtration system for incoming and outgoing air. There are special filtration systems on the market designed just for this purpose (see page 50).

A *microwave oven* for warming up diets is, of course, indispensable (but see the warning on page 93), together with a three or four ring *gas or electric cooking range* or some *heating elements* that are so constructed or installed that lively youngsters cannot touch them. You must have boiling water available for the sterilization of *feeding utensils* (tubes, syringes, bent spoons, crop needles, food bowls, etc.). Cold sterilization exists, but the equipment for this method is very expensive.

During egg-handling or chick-feeding sessions, it is highly recommended that you always wear a "fresh" face mask and rubber gloves so that you reduce the possibilities of transmitting diseases caused by harmful microorganisms such as bacteria, viruses, chlamydia, and yeast. You know the proverb: "An ounce of prevention is worth a pound of cure." The application of strict hygienic practices will drastically reduce the possibilities of infection problems.

One or more *bird intensive care units* or *hospital units* for sick or injured chicks is essential. Such units will be frequently used as nursery units for hand-raised young

Hospital cage.

birds and are, next to the incubator, the most important equipment.

A few *electronic digital thermometers* are no superfluous luxury, as the mercury thermometers in incubators and intensive care units are not always reliable. Such thermometers are also useful for testing the temperatures of warmed diets. Remember: sick birds are always quarantined outside the main nursery.

A *container* (frequently an old aquarium) can be used when feeding chicks or to keep them in while they wait their turn. In such cases, a *heat lamp* can be used to provide extra warmth.

Different kinds of *candlers* are also necessary. There are models that can be placed in the nest of the brooding bird; other models can be used when inspecting the eggs in an incubator. We use the term "candlers" because, "in the old days," gamekeepers did indeed use wax candles to inspect the eggs of pheasants and similar birds.

One or more sets of *scales* are essential, as we shall see (see page 113), for the regular weighing of the chicks. Eggs should lose moisture during incubation and it is advisable to keep a check on their weight. As well as simple scales, *electronic scales* are available; these are more accurate and thus suitable for egg weighing.

A few *notebooks* are extremely important to keep such necessary records as chick and egg weights.

In a separate *cabinet*, we keep our medical supplies—if you have children, keep the supplies under lock and key—and in another cabinet we keep our various cleaning materials (see page 46).

Once you get busy raising young birds in a small corner of a room, you will soon have to consider moving into a separate breeding room, or a building in the yard. In that case, it is highly recommended that the walls and ceilings be covered with easily *washable and disinfectable material*—to make everyone happy!

Some good transportable *lamps* are important, so that you can see what you are doing and what you must do, such as properly handfeeding, reading thermometers for the correct diet temperature, and so on. In this connection we can add to our list of equipment a *blender* or *food processor*, and a large number of *uniform, airtight plastic containers* for our hand-feeding diets. I mention "uniform" containers, as they will be stored in a refrigerator or freezer and will therefore pack more efficiently.

We should keep sufficient bottles of *distilled (spring) water* in the refrigerator; most commercial diets recommend the use of this water in their mixtures.

You might say to yourself, "What a huge list!" But there will be even more items we may require as we get busy; for example, some *hand towels* (not too wooly or the birds will get their claws caught in them) can be used to place the chicks on when they are being fed. They can also be used on the floor of an intensive care or nursery unit. Some *paper kitchen towels* or *napkins* are useful for cleaning the chicks' beaks, faces, feet, and bodies (I like to use *soft toilet tissue* for this).

One important item I have left until last. You know that we have several items controlled by the main electrical power. When we have to rely on electrical power coming from one source, it is, for me, at any rate, a constant, nerve-racking worry, because, if there should be a power failure, and we have eggs in the incubator and chicks in the nursery, it can be disastrous! A *backup power generator* is thus essential. Do not attempt to install such a unit or do any other major electrical repairs or alterations yourself unless you know exactly what you are doing. For the sake of safety, call in a professional electrician. In many states, only licensed professionals are allowed to do such work anyway. Your local electricity supply company will advise you on what you can and cannot do.

Human infant incubator, an excellent brooder for all types of birds.

Finally, on pages 6–8 we discussed egg repairs in detail; we thus also require "*tools*" for this task. Make it a rule to keep all such tools in a *single container*, so that you don't have to search all over the house each time you need them! The essential items for egg repair are:

- glue
- scissors
- bandage
- sterile water (for cleaning eggshell or young after feeding)
- cotton balls (same)
- gauze
- cotton swabs (for moistening of egg membranes while chick is trying to hatch; also for cleaning the young after feeding)
- silver nitrate sticks (for example, to cauterize active blood vessels,

Three-week-old African Gray Parrots.

and to stop bleeding. There is a commercial brand available in the United States called Quick-Stop, but this does not work as well as the cheaper silver nitrate sticks)

- tweezers (useful in helping young hatch from the egg, see page 8)
- Betadine solution 1% (mainly used to treat the umbilius, see page 7)
- and Betadine Scrub or a similar product (against some viruses, fungi, and bacteria, and mainly used to scrub hands before handling eggs or young
- I also advise the use of rubber gloves (as discussed, see page 6), which are also washed in this product much in the same way as washing your hands.)

Cages

As bird breeders you will need an adequate quantity of *cages*. You will need these when young birds leave their nursery and must "stand on

their own legs." It is therefore important that you have enough cages to house the young you are raising, and bear in mind that, if you are raising several species, many of these cannot be housed together. Additionally, overcrowding in cages can soon lead to a disease outbreak. While hand-raising, we always keep only birds of a single species together in the same nursery unit; in other words, from day one until fully grown, we keep, for example African Gray Parrots together, Amazon species together (Blue-fronted Amazons with Blue-fronted Amazons, White-fronted Amazons with White-fronted Amazons, and so on), and the same goes for cockatoos, macaws, etc.

Sanitation

At the present time, hand-feeding baby birds can no longer be regarded as a seasonal activity. Some breeders even raise baby birds throughout the year, although I doubt that it is a responsible thing to do!

In such cases, I am not only concerned about the "laying-hen" degraded, egg-producing, mother bird, but also about the impossibility of daily sanitizing the bird nursery and all its equipment at set times, or of applying a fresh coat of paint. As a breeder, you may think it is profitable to sell baby birds for 365 days of the year, but such an operation can be doomed quicker than you may think. Sanitation and/or disinfection in the bird nursery is of the greatest importance, as baby birds are incredibly vulnerable to a wide range of diseases. (In Chapter 9 we will discuss some of these in detail.) Therefore, if at a given moment you have no baby birds to care for, or only a few that can be temporarily housed elsewhere, put your shoulders to the wheel, put rubber gloves on your hands, cover your nose and mouth with a surgical mask—and clean and disinfect!

You think that "outfit" is somewhat overdone? Believe me, you do need to protect yourself. Many breeders who have not protected themselves as suggested have succumbed to chemical reactions caused by the frequently toxic chemicals used for disinfection. A case that I am aware of illustrates the point admirably: An overzealous fancier was convinced that there were innumerable viruses, bacteria, and such lurking in every corner, ready to attack and destroy her baby birds! In addition to the rest of her nursery, she decided to spray the acoustic ceiling tiles. Her intention was good, but the manner in which she did it is not recommended. She set out to spray every square inch of the ceiling with neat gluteraldehyde. She was so absorbed in her task that she failed to notice the tiny, microscopic droplets falling onto her face, or being breathed into her lungs! Suddenly she was overcome with nausea, she began to vomit, and lost the feeling in her arms. A visit to the

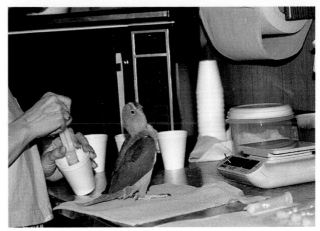

A hungry Alexandrine Parrot (Psittacula eupatria nipalensis). Note the scale on the right.

emergency room and many phone calls to doctors, poison control centers, and chemical manufacturers, as well as great family concern, were the direct consequences! Luckily, after a terrible week, she recovered completely. Of course, no single virus, or lurking bacillus would have survived her attack on them, but the way it was done left much to be desired.

We can make two important points from this story: It pays to wear protective gear, and, before you start to spray, make sure that you have followed the manufacturer's directions regarding mixing and dilution. Don't think like the man whose doctor prescribed two pills a day for a week—he swallowed them all at once, and wondered why he was sicker than he has been in the first place! Particular directions by the manufacturer are designed to be followed.

Disinfectants

Most available disinfectants are sold in concentrated form and must be diluted before use. These disinfectants are tested and qualified in the dilutions stated on the label. Environmental Protection Agency labeling is very effective and specific, and you are strongly advised to strictly obey the instructions. If the label says use one part concentrated disinfectant diluted with 16, 32, or 64 parts water, then do just that! The disinfectant will do the job. A stronger solution won't kill any more germs, bacteria, viruses, or other pests—it will only be more hazardous for you, the user.

I will suggest the names of some disinfectants (see page 49), but first this: during the Midwest Avian Research Expo in 1993, Dr. Sam Vaughn, B.S., D.V.M., presented a paper that I here (pages 46–52) paraphrase:

"Disinfection is the act of destroying many of the disease-causing microorganisms [present on the surface of an inanimate object] such as viruses, bacteria, yeast, chlamydia, and mycoplasma that contaminate utensils and surfaces. Many of us, however, barely consider that disinfectants are toxic (i.e., poisonous). Indeed, those disinfectants used by veterinarians and aviculturists are potentially dangerous. In extensive testing to determine which disinfectants are effective against PBFD virus and Polyoma virus, Branson Ritchie, D.V.M., Ph. D., discovered that many disinfectants are so toxic that they destroy the medium in which the viruses are cultured, making it impossible to reach a conclusive result."

How to Clean and Disinfect

Let us have a look at what we can do to thoroughly clean and disinfect our nursery, cages, and aviaries. We know that many bacterial and fungal diseases may originate from environmental sources. It is thus important to eliminate these sources, as part of an overall therapeutic plan; otherwise, there is a chance that our birds will be continually reinfected, even those that may have been successfully treated with antimicrobial drugs previously.

If you feed your birds fruit and vegetables or soft foods (universal/egg foods), these must *not* be returned to the refrigerator if they have been in the open air (perhaps in the nursery, cage, or aviary) longer than 24 hours. Such foods will spoil quickly in higher temperatures (such as in the incubator, where you shouldn't really put food anyway). Commercial universal or soft egg foods (CéDé, for example) are especially common sources of pseudomonas; fruits and vegetables are a source of gram negative bacteria and yeast.

With regard to commercial food, poor storage can result in large numbers of potentially harmful bacteria, such as *Escherichia coli*, doing untold damage (see Bacterial Diseases, page 130). It has also become apparent that monkey chow, which was (and is) used extensively in the preparation of hand-feeding diets, may yield—although not documented as yet—large numbers of yeast spores. Dry dog foods and pelleted bird diets are probably a better choice.

Much attention should be given to the cleaning of feeding and other utensils. Gram negative bacteria and yeast are commonly isolated from utensils, blenders, syringes, cutting boards, work benches, etc., which are never scrupulously cleaned and disinfected after use. It is thus obvious that all unclean utensils open the possibility of contaminating each new food batch, with all the troublesome consequences this can cause.

As we are also discussing natural breeding in this book, I would recommend that after each breeding season, once the young have left the nest and are fully independent, the nest material be removed from the nest boxes and burned. Pine shavings and other material used as bedding in the baby room should also be burned after use, as they can carry *Klebsiella*. High numbers of yeast spores and various fungi can be found in peat moss. Never use damp or wet bedding materials; these only provide an excellent breeding ground for all kinds of fungal growth.

We use a lot of water in our hobby: for preparing baby foods; for washing utensils, blenders, etc.; for cleaning incubators, cages, and work tops; for filling the drinking fountains in aviaries and cages;

and so on. If you use a garden hose to fill drink and bath containers in the aviary, it is recommended that they be replaced with a new one each season as it is apparent that they can harbor *Pseudomonas* and *Aeromonas* (see page 141) organisms. Beware—the same applies to drinkers and commercial bottled water dispensers, leading to the question of what do we use—tap water or bottled water? Personally, alas, after hearing and reading various reports on the radio or in newspapers, I no longer have any great reliance on bottled water. One must especially pay attention to the experiences of other breeders. One of them, a very professional and experienced breeder, was confronted in 1995 with babies that were sick with bacterial infections. Various medications didn't help (or hardly helped), and the babies got sick again with whatever was making them sick in the first place. The breeder realized that something was definitely wrong with the diet or the environment. He tested all and everything in his establishment. Eventually, he tested the water bottles and, bingo! various bottles contained *E. coli*, some in the caps, some in the water itself! This breeder now takes no more risks, and boils all the water he uses. In this connection, I would advise that before tap water is used as drinking water, or for cleaning the nursery, the water be allowed to run for a while to flush out any bacteria that may be lurking in the tap itself. If you happen to use well water, you should have it tested from time to time for coliform contamination.

My tip: Most birds quickly learn how to drink from automatic drip waterers or bottle waterers (similar to those used for laboratory animals). By using such utensils, we not only eliminate spillage (which will also prevent food, bedding, etc. from becoming wet), but also the possibility of contamination. Open drinking vessels should be cleaned and disinfected daily. *Pseudomonas* is regarded as the most frequent contaminator of automatic watering systems, and especially those made from PVC (polyvinyl chloride.)

Those who have several aviaries or nurseries frequently make use of one or more foot baths to decontaminate their rubber boots. Of course, this will only be effective if the disinfectant in the foot bath (square or rectangular metal containers with a height of about 7 inches [17.5 cm]) is renewed at regular intervals, as dictated by its label, otherwise, contamination (*Pseudomonas*, in particular) is not out of the question each time the foot bath is used.

It is important to maintain the temperature and relative humidity as constant as possible in the nursery. A warm, moist environment is ideal for the development of fungi and bacteria. The addition of vitamin supplements to drinking water also encourages bacterial growth; therefore the following rules will apply:

1. Replace drinking water at least once a day, especially if vitamins are dissolved in it.
2. Water vessels should be thoroughly scrubbed and disinfected at least three times a week.
3. Feeding vessels for soft foods, fruits, and vegetables should be cleaned and disinfected daily.
4. Feeding vessels for commercial seed mixes and pellets should be cleaned and disinfected once a week; foreign particles should be removed from the seed, especially clumps of seed arising as a result of damp or droppings.

My tip: Number feeding and watering vessels with a black marker and always use the same vessels for the same cages, aviaries, nurseries, etc. to reduce chances of cross infections.

Finally, what do we do if we should experience an outbreak of an infectious disease? Of course, the first step must be to try to find and eliminate the source of the infection by thorough cleaning and disinfection. Remember that many viruses, bacteria, chlamydia, and fungi can survive for weeks, even years, in, for example, dry fecal matter, and even successfully treated birds can thus be reinfected. Therefore, the birds should be placed in separate accommodations while the nursery is thoroughly cleaned and disinfected. With viral infections, the best remedy is to remove and burn all items that are difficult to sterilize (such as wooden perches, nest boxes, feeders, toys, etc.). Obviously, any food that has been exposed to the sick birds must be removed and burned.

Case Report

Various breeders have warned me about the water sources derived from the Rocky Mountain snow runoff. There are days when my telephone is almost glowing red with calls reporting cases of baby birds infected with giardia; breeders from Colorado and New Mexico are particularly affected. As you probably know, giardia is considered to be a health hazard, and all water districts constantly monitor their supplies in attempts to keep this parasite under control, but not always with success. Many breeders who use well water also have found giardia in their supply. All too often incubator-hatched chicks examined by veterinarians are diagnosed with giardia infection. Everything points in the direction of the snow water from the Rocky Mountains! Fortunately, we can get the better of this parasite but it must be diagnosed and treated specifically, because commonly used broad-spectrum drugs are of no help.

My tip: Never take your water's purity for granted. Try to ascertain what is good and what is bad in your water supply; have it tested regularly. Indeed, water is the elixir of all life, and the single most essential item that we and our baby birds require.

Some Effective Disinfectants

Chlorinated compounds: The best known is sodium hypochloride, or simply bleach. It is available in liquid form, such as Clorox and Purex, or as a stabilized powder. A 1:32 solution (half cup per gallon [3.79 L] of water) is adequate for most purposes, especially if used in sunlight and diluted in soft water. It will kill almost all viruses, bacteria, mycoplasmas, and probably chlamydia. It should be used in adequately ventilated areas and the user is advised to wear eye protection and gloves.

Chlorhexidine gluconates: Various brand names are available including Novassan, Hibitane, Virosan, and Hibistat. In addition to being used as a skin antiseptic, these can be used as an inanimate-surface disinfectant. I would certainly recommend them as a brooder and incubator water additive, for the control of fungal growth, especially *Aspergillus*. They are also effective against other fungi, bacteria, yeast, and various viruses (including Newcastle virus). They can even be added to our birds' drinking water. They are not very efficient against gram negative bacteria including *Pseudomonas*. Virosan and Novassan are both chlorhexidine; neither is effective against *Pseudomonas,* nor are they effective against bacterial spores or *Mycobacterium*.

Formalin: This is used extensively in Europe, though in the United States its use is mainly confined to laboratories. Formalin is a 40 percent solution of formaldehyde and is not expensive but, unfortunately, it is difficult to obtain due to U.S. government regulations. It kills practically all bacteria, spores, fungi, tuberculosis, and several viruses. The fumes, however, are extremely dangerous, and it is caustic to skin and mucous membranes on contact, or with vapor inhalation. Beware: Fumigatory gases from formaldehyde and Km No. 4 are lethal to germs, animals, and humans!

Phenols: Sodium orthophenol is sold in combination with cleaners and several disinfectants. Various products, including Lysol, LPH, One Stroke Environ, O-Syl, Staphene and Matar Amerse are available in grocery stores and most pet shops. One Stroke Environ is used by the United States Drug Administration for cleaning quarantine stations at the rate of 1 ounce per gallon (3.79 L) of water. Phenols kill various pathogens including bacteria (*Pseudomonas*, *Salmonella*), fungi, tuberculosis *bacilli,* and *lipohillica* viruses. You are advised to wear goggles and gloves when using these products; it is also corrosive to tissues. Phenols are particularly toxic to cats and to other animals, such as reptiles.

Gluteraldehydes: Well-known trademarks include: Wavecide, Sterol, Banacide, Spocide, Sonacide, Cybact, Cidex, and MC-25. The most important function of the chemical is to denature both DNA and RNA protein. It is generally thought to be very effective against all tested pathogens; herpes viruses, for example, were killed in ten seconds. In 1962, Johnson & Johnson brought Cidex onto the market, but ten years later, acid gluteraldehyhe monomers were introduced. The modern gluteraldehydes are considerably more stable and have a longer life. Tests have shown that they will destroy the human venereal chlamydia organism. At present, it is not known if they will control *Chlamydia psittaci,* although tests to date have proven promising. Unfortunately, it is not readily available, and purchase without a medical license is often not possible, but many avian veterinarians can supply it to their clients.

Air Cleaners

After rearing baby birds for a year or two, most breeders find that they need to make changes and improvements in their facilities. For example, we may find that the workbench would be better against another wall, perhaps beneath a window, or it would be nice to have a second refrigerator, if only we had enough power sources. In short, after a while, we will know what works and what doesn't work in our nursery, and the time for carpentry, rewiring, and/or plumbing will begin again. Regarding sanitation, we must be sure that *every* surface must be easy to sanitize; it is essential to use hard surfaces such as tile, enamel, formica, stainless steel, and vinyl wall coverings. One of my first improvements, in fact, during my first breeding season, was the installation of a commercial air cleaner. Although I clean it out daily, I am always amazed at the amount of matter it filters out of the air: feather dust and particles, down feather shafts, greasy dust, and who knows what else? A white filter becomes a black one practically overnight! And it is a fact that airborne diseases can travel on all of the above-named debris. An air cleaner, in fact, has a three-fold function: It controls the dust, provides quality air, and traps germs. I wouldn't be without one (see pages 144–145)!

If you decide to obtain an air cleaner, shop around, as there are many models, of various qualities, to choose from (see pages 144–145). Study the literature, and ask questions (most manufacturers have an 800-number). Give preference to air cleaners that filter out a high percentage (preferably 95 percent or better) of viruses, bacteria, and fungi. Consider the cost of maintenance, and especially calculate the cost of regular (daily, if possible) replacement of filters. Replacement must occur more often than in "usual" use. Our baby bird nursery requires the air to be as clean as possible to prevent disease outbreaks. And remember that even the most expensive air filter will be useless if it has to run with dirty filters.

As I said, I have been extremely satisfied with my air cleaner. My electric bill was not greatly affected, and the fan does an excellent job circulating the air, ensuring a comfortable temperature in the nursery and brooders throughout the year.

The aviculturist should be aware that basic sanitation in the nursery is far more significant than the choice of disinfectant. Used improperly, and sometimes even when the manufacturer's instructions are followed implicitly, disinfectants can be dangerously toxic to you and your birds. The only way for a veterinarian to discover the source of repeated bacterial infections in an aviary or nursery is to carefully supervise the premises, review the records, and monitor routine daily maintenance. The most frequent source of bacterial or yeast contamination in breeding pairs occurs in the water bowl and in moist food. Water bottles are much preferred, as the water cannot be contaminated with feces, and the birds cannot get food into it, which provides the "bacterial tea" that is far too common in the cage and aviary situation.

Bacteria

To prevent fecal contamination of food (in an aviary, for example), feeding vessels should be placed at, or above, perch level. Covers can also be placed over the feeding vessels to produce similar results. My cleanest avicultural friend employs the feeding habits of his parrots to minimize bacterial load. Feeding the birds twice daily, he removes all uneaten food two hours later, thus ensuring minimum spoilage and fecal contamination. As they would in the wild, his parrots feed at dawn and dusk, a regimen that suits them very well.

Bacteria are one of life's necessities and it is not possible to maintain a completely sterile aviary or nursery. Our birds harbor normal bacteria (often called "normal flora") in their bodies and to persistently use disinfectants or antibiotics in food or water to try to keep birds healthy is counterproductive. All we will achieve by doing this is to create strains of bacteria that are resistant to all available antibiotics. Some of my avicultural friends often become frustrated because I refuse to sell them antibiotics, because to do so would make me their birds' worst enemy. The best course is to visit the aviary and make *management* changes necessary to prevent bacterial recontamination. Only then is it possible to successfully eradicate infection in an aviary.

Quarantine of any new additions to an aviary is far more important than disinfection. Examine your existing stock for PBFD and polyoma virus in order to know who is clean, and add no birds to the aviary until they have undergone appropriate quarantine and testing procedures. Cultures on new additions may prevent introduction of bacterially infected birds into your clean stock.

Thus, disinfection, i.e., sanitation, is not of paramount importance. The most important tools at your disposal are management and education. Keep in mind these simple things:

- wash your hands with antibacterial soap between babies or groups of babies;
- clean syringes and other feeding utensils properly after each use and store in a disinfectant solution;
- clean food and water bowls routinely;
- do not expose your nursery to adult birds either by air or traffic from the aviary to the nursery (foot baths are invaluable).

The answer to infectious disease problems is management, testing, and vaccination, not toxic chemicals that people use to try to kill bacteria in a filthy environment.

Banding Chicks

It doesn't matter what methods we use to breed our birds, whether in a cage, an aviary, or an incubator, or what species we breed, as long as we provide our breeding birds with leg bands. Various avicultural organizations provide rings for their members. The rings (so-called closed rings or bands) are marked with the organization's identity mark, the member's breeder number, year of issue, and a serial number. The rings come in various sizes (see pages 55–58), and there is a ring to fit every species we may breed.

When to Leg Band

The time for leg banding varies, but averages about the seventh day, with the exception of larger parrot species. Canaries are best banded when the chicks' droppings start to pile up around the rim of the nest, indicating that the parent birds are no longer removing them. If you band the chicks earlier, there is always the chance that the parent birds will regard the ring as a "foreign body" in the nest and throw it out, complete with the nestling to which it is attached! Also, if you band your birds too early, there is a chance that the ring will work itself loose during all the activity going on in the nest. If the birds are too old, the foot may be too big to take the correct ring. You can try lubricating the foot with Vaseline or a little salad oil (*but don't forget to clean it off when you're finished*) to help the ring slip over the foot. On no account use brute force! If it won't go, then stop; we don't want an invalid bird!

The cleaner the parent birds are, the more difficult it is to leg band the youngsters. There is, however, a compromise course you can take. In most cases, the bands are made of aluminum, stainless steel, or copper, and are more or less shiny. We can take the gloss off the band by using a felt-tipped pen; then they are no longer so conspicuous. Also, if new rings are left in sunlight for a few weeks, they will lose their shine.

Most ringing is best done toward evening, when the hens are not working so busily and there is less danger of them throwing the freshly banded young out of the nest. If all is in order the next morning, you

Closed bird bands (rings) come in different sizes.

can be sure your banding has been successful.

How to Leg Band

Though it sounds somewhat unhygienic, you should perform your leg banding with "dirty" hands! Just pull up a bunch of grass and rub your hands into it. That way, you will get rid of your human smell, which could upset the birds. Be careful not to damage nests when removing birds, especially nests built in a bunch of hay, or a shrub, in an aviary.

Hold the bird, belly upward, in the palm of the hand and take one of its legs between your thumb and forefinger, just at the foot joint. With the other hand, push the ring over the three forward directed toes. It may be that the three toes are difficult to hold together, in which case you can stick them in your mouth and moisten them with saliva—that usually does the trick. Take care that the three toes all go through the ring. Hold the ring on the ball of the foot, and, holding the three toes, push the ring onto the leg as far as it will go. Then, with the aid of a matchstick (or something similar), pull out the back toe, and that's that!

Parrots and parakeets have toes designed for climbing; two are directed forward, and two backward. We band these birds in the same way except that the ring is first passed over the forward two toes, then the backward pair.

Many novices believe leg banding to be difficult. They are worried that they may damage the tiny toes of the nestlings, hurt them, or upset the whole breeding process. It is not so difficult if you think about it carefully, and go about it with confidence. Once you have done it a few times, you will be able to breeze through it. It only needs a little practice to become skillful.

At your first banding attempt you should be without spectators, or you may become nervous and embarrassed. Many people find it creepy, children feel pity, and the aviculturist perspires profusely!

Why Leg Banding Is Necessary

Why is leg banding necessary? Well, in the first place we can tell if the ringed bird is from our own breeding stock. As long as we use the correct ring, there is little danger of the bird losing it once it has left the nest. With regard to "closed" rings, it is impossible to use the same size on an adult. It can only be applied when the feet are small and the toes still supple.

The band tells us in which year the bird was born, and if we keep a record of our births and band serial numbers, we will know the exact date of birth and the identity of the parents. Banded birds have certain advantages at exhibitions where the bands prove the breeding and ownership of a particular breeder. There is no art in exhibiting a newly bought bird! There are a few exceptions among birds that are difficult to keep in good condition, let alone breed them. In Europe, tanagers, for example, fit into this category.

Closed banding is also important with an eye to the future. It is not out of the question that, before long, all captive-bred birds shipped interstate or from country to country will be required to be closed banded to help quell the illegal wild bird trade. Of course, there are "open" rings that can be applied to the legs of adult birds with the aid of special pliers. Breeders of large species, zoos, and bird parks often use this method to identify their birds. Cocks, for example, may be banded on the right leg, hens on the left. Colored plastic bands are also available (mainly for smaller birds such as finches and canaries) and are used, especially in Europe, to identify sexes, year of birth, and so on. Microchip implants are also available for identifying baby birds. Ask your avian veterinarian for more details.

Record Keeping

I have referred several times to "record keeping." With the breeding of many domesticated birds (parakeets, cockatiels, canaries, Zebra Finches, lovebirds, etc.), and expensive species, such as Hooded Siskins, Hyacynthine Macaws, Queen's Conures, or various Amazon parrots, it is essential that we know from which parents they came, how the young were raised, if the breeding pair was reliable, and what we might expect of the young in regard to color, form, and carriage. Were they well raised, or were there difficulties? Were there any genetic abnormalities? In short, any facts (and not only breeding facts) that may become useful to us in the future should be recorded. It is quite impossible to remember everything, especially if you're breeding many pairs of birds. So, "bookkeeping" is an essential part of our hobby and you can make your register as comprehensive as you like.

Apart from the information you may need for the next breeding season (to achieve the right pairings, for example), your records will also supply useful information for any purchaser of your birds. Everybody has the right to know what they are buying!

On the following page is a concise register card of the type I use.

Band Sizes

It is also important to keep a record of band sizes. Here is a guide

Banding your birds is essential!

to ring sizes for various species. These sizes should be considered approximate sizes for an average bird, as listed below. Diameter (in millimeters) is the internal ring/band measurement.

2.0 mm Orange-cheeked Waxbill, Red-eared Waxbill, Crimson Waxbill, St. Helena Waxbill, Red-cheeked Cordon Bleu, Red Avadavat, and birds of similar size.

2.3 mm Crimson-winged Waxbill (Aurora Finch), Melba Finch, all *Erytrura* (parrot finch) species, Violet-eared Waxbill, Common Quail Finch, Double-barred Finch, Red-tailed Lavender Finch, Indian Silverbill, African Silverbill, Pearl-headed Silverbill, Spice Finch, Long-tailed Finch, Masked Finch, Gouldian Finch, Pintailed Parrot Finch, all American siskin species, and bird species of a similar size.

Table 3
Register Card

Breeding Card No: ....

Season: 19 ....

Cage (aviary/incubator) No. ....

Bird Species ....

Ring No. Male: .... Born: .... Color: ....

Ring No. Female: .... Born: .... Color: ....

Batch No. 1   **Particular details**

Date first egg: ....

Total eggs (clutch): ....

Date of brooding: ....

Date of hatching: ....

No. hatched birds: ....

Banded: ....

Batch No. 2   **Particular details**

Date first egg: ....

Total eggs (clutch): ....

Date of brooding: ....

Date of hatching: ....

No. hatched birds: ....

Banded: ....

Batch No. 3   **Particular details**

Date first egg: ....

Total eggs (clutch): ....

Date of brooding: ....

Date of hatching: ....

No. hatched birds: ....

Banded: ....

2.5 mm Cut-throat Finch, Red-headed Finch, Chestnut-breasted Finch, Society Finch, Diamond Sparrow, and bird species of a similar size.

2.9 mm Song-, color-, and various posture (form-) canaries, Common Bullfinch, Greenfinch, Saffron Finch, Black-headed Canary (Alario

Table 4
Bands Provided Exclusively by the AFA[*]

Size	Species
9/32″	Gold-capped, Jendaya, and Sun Conures
5/16″	Caiques, Hawk-headed Parrot, *Pionus* species, small mini-macaws, White-fronted Amazon, Yellow-lored Amazon, Mitred Conure, Red-fronted Conure, and White-eyed Conure
3/8″	Citron-crested Cockatoo, Goffin's Cockatoo, large mini-macaws, Lesser Sulpher-crested Cockatoo, Yellow-faced Amazon, Yellow-shouldered Amazon
7/16″	African Gray Parrot, Blue-fronted Amazon, Lilac-crowned Amazon, Medium Sulphur-crested Cockatoo, Orange-winged Amazon, Red-headed Amazon, Red-lored Amazon, and some Lesser Sulphur-crested Cockatoos
1/2″	Blue-crowned Amazon, Greater Sulphur-crested Cockatoo, large Double Yellow-headed Amazon, large Yellow-naped Amazon, Mealy Amazon, Military Macaw, Moluccan Cockatoo, Red-fronted Macaw, Umbrella Cockatoo, Yellow-crowned Amazon.
9/16″	Blue and Gold Macaw, Scarlet Macaw
5/8″	Buffon's Macaw, large Green-winged Macaw and Hyacinth Macaw
3/16″	Cockatiels, Lovebirds, some Rosellas

[*]In an effort to promote record keeping and management programs, the American Federation of Aviculture (AFA) is offering a way to mark your unbanded birds. Psittacine bands constructed of 300 series stainless steel (the same as being used by USDA quarantine stations) are available from 3/16″ to 9/32″ in any quantity. All bands are stamped with a unique AFA code and are, therefore, traceable. Plastic bandettes (1/8″ for canaries, 5/32″ for budgies, and 1/14″ for cockatiels) are also available.

Finch), various tanager species, and bird species of a similar size.

3.5 mm Java Sparrow (Rice Bird), Pekin Robin, bulbul species, Shama Thrush, Norwich, Yorkshire, and Lancashire canaries, and bird species of a similar size.

4.0 mm Budgerigar (parakeet), cardinal species, small tropical doves and quail, *Neophema* species, *Forpus* species, and bird species of a similar size.

4.5 mm Lovebirds, small lories and lorikeets, hanging (*Loriculus*) parakeets, and bird species of a similar size.

5.4 mm Cockatiel, Plum-headed Parakeet, Kakariki, Hooded Parrot,

Red-rumped Parakeet, Aymora Parakeet, Stanley Rosella, small *Pyrrhura* species, larger doves, and bird species of similar size.

6.0 mm Large doves and pigeons, quail, all larger rosellas, Moustached Parakeet, Monk Parakeet, Princess of Wales Parakeet, *Barnardius* species, *Trichoglossus* species, large *Pyrrhura* species, Ringneck Parakeet, Peach-fronted Conure, White-eared Conure, and bird species of a similar size.

7.0 mm Australian crowned doves and Australian bronze-winged doves (pigeons).

8.0 mm Chukar Partridge.

10.0 mm Carolona Duck, Golden Pheasant, and birds of a similar size.

12.0 mm Larger pheasants (e.g., Silver Pheasant); the largest pheasant species should be banded with 14 mm bands.

The three grays and one dilute Cockatiels were all from the same brood.

Chapter Four
Incubation

What You Need to Know About Incubation

The reproduction of the species is the most important driving force of all animals. In most cases two partners are necessary: a male and a female. Copulation and fertilization are the first two events that must take place before the species can multiply. In the male bird, there are two papillae on the rudimentary copulatory organ. During copulation, these papillae are filled with lymph and thus enlarged. Sperm flows along a groove in the rounded copulatory organ. The copulatory organ can be recognized even in day-old chicks of ducks, chickens, and ratites (ostriches, emus, etc.), making these birds relatively easy to sex at an early age.

During copulation, which usually takes only a few seconds, the *cloacae* of the male and female birds turn out and are pressed together. The male spermatozoa then flow out into the oviduct of the female where they are stored in a reservoir. At intervals, they make their way through the oviduct to the funnel-shaped entrance of the oviduct called the *infundibulum*. When a ripe ovum bursts from the ovary during ovulation, one of the spermatozoa in the funnel forces through the egg cell membrane and fertilization takes place. During the further development of the egg, when albumen is deposited on the yolk, the yolk membrane becomes denser. In this connection, it is interesting to note that *parthenogenesis* sometimes occurs in turkeys, that is, reproduction without fertilized eggs.

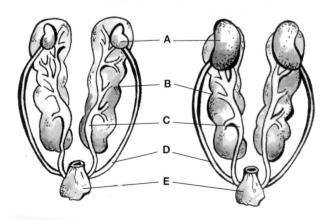

The enlargement of the male testes during the breeding season: A. Testes; B. Kidney; C. Ureter; D. Vas deferens; and E. Cloaca.

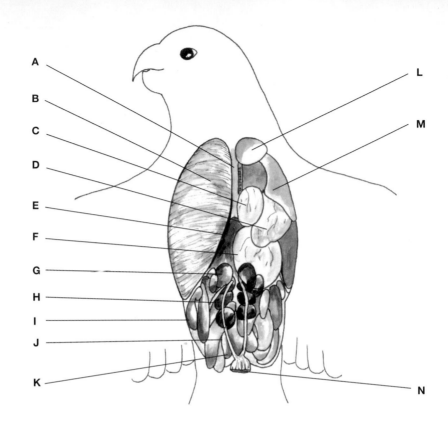

Brooding Birds

As soon as the eggs are laid, the third reproductory phase of the species begins. The bird becomes "broody," in that the feeling of the eggs against the breast stimulates the release of the hormone *prolactine* in the bloodstream.

Birds that lay only a single egg normally begin to brood directly after laying. With birds that lay several eggs, there are some that start brooding after the last egg is laid (as we see in ducks, geese, and many small songbirds). Others, such as pelicans, owls, hummingbirds, various finches and waxbills, and some parrots begin to brood after the first, second, or third egg of clutch. A brooding bird leaves the nest only a few times a day; a pheasant, for example, spends at about one hour a day away from the nest in order to feed. Several thrush species leave the nest about 20

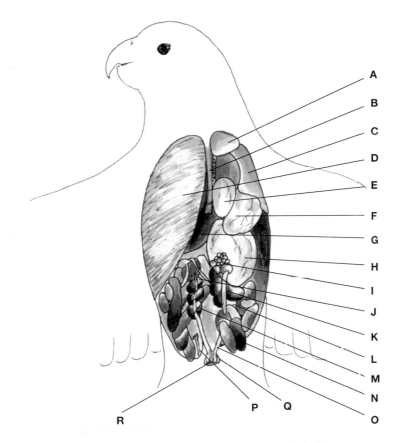

Female Anatomy
A. Crop
B. Sternum
C. Air sacs
D. Breast and
   flight muscles
E. Heart
F. Liver (left lobe)
G. Liver (right
   lobe)
H. Gizzard
I. Ovary
J. Right
   kidney
K. Infundibulum
L. Left oviduct
M. Ureter
N. Isthmus
O. Uterus
P. Rudimentary
   right oviduct
Q. Vagina
R. Cloaca

times a day, while hummingbirds, which cannot store much energy in their tiny bodies, must leave the nest at least 100 times a day to feed.

Which Ones Brood— Male or Female?

In many songbirds, ducks, geese, owls, hummingbirds, and sunbirds, only the hen does the brooding. The cock bird stays in the neighborhood of the nest and regularly brings his mate food. With kiwis, tinamous,

rheas, emus, casuaries, and king penguins, only the male does the brooding. Both sexes brood among the cockatoos, with the exception of the black cockatoos, where only the females brood. But here there is also an exception—both sexes of the Palm Cockatoo sometimes brood the eggs.

When both partners brood, the male usually does so during the day, the female at night, but the hen often takes longer shifts than her partner. An exception can be found in many waterfowl where the drake and duck perform more or less equal shifts on the nest. With doves and Black Swans, the male broods from about 10:00 A.M. until 5:00 P.M.; then the female takes over. Starling couples relieve each other from the nest several times a day, but only the hen broods at night. Woodpeckers behave similarly, but here the male broods overnight. The dark-colored male Ostrich also broods at night. Some astrilds relieve each other day and night.

Brooding Eggs

Brooding eggs means "to transfer the warmth of the body to the eggs." The breast feathers of the brooding birds are so arranged that the naked skin of the brood spots comes into direct contact with the eggs. The brood spot is richly supplied with surface blood vessels, so that maximum warmth can be transferred to the eggs. The down feathers on the breast are shed from the brood spots at brooding time, and the skin of the breast becomes spongy in texture. Depending on the species, birds either have no, one, or more brood spots. Ducks, geese, cormorants, and penguins, for example, do not have brood spots; most songbirds, grebes, and doves have one brood spot; auks, two; gulls, three. The bare patches on the breasts of brooding ducks and geese are the result of the birds plucking out the down themselves.

Temperature

The body temperature of a non-breeding chicken averages 104.9°F (40.5°C). At brooding time, this sinks to around 102.2°F (39°C). The part of the egg that contacts the hen's body has a temperature of 84.6°F (29.2°C). The male King Penguin broods when the Antarctic temperature is as low as –76°F (–60°C), but his body temperature averages 93.2°F (34°C) plus. He must brood without food for about eight weeks in this harsh environment.

The temperature measured in the brood spot of a brooding pheasant is 103.1°F (39.5°C); the upper surface of the brooded egg has a temperature of 95°F (35°C), the lower surface 77°F (25°C). The temperature difference between the upper and lower surfaces of the egg reduces as the embryo develops and itself begins to produce warmth. The eggs are regularly turned and rolled backward and forward. A domestic hen, for example, turns her eggs about every half hour during the day, every one to two hours at night. That is about 30 times a day. Egg turning prevents the embryo from adhering to the egg membrane, which would be fatal. The brooding bird changes position frequently so that all eggs are warmed equally throughout the brooding period. The embryo sits on the upper surface of the yolk, so that it is as close as possible to the source of warmth. An egg lays with its pointed end toward the center of the nest, so that the blunt end, where the air sac is situated, lays somewhat higher.

Feeding the Young

The period of incubation depends on the species (see page 12). Once the young have hatched, there are two possibilities (see pages 18–19): the nest leavers (precocial) can go out with their parents to seek food shortly after hatching; they are soon independent and have an instinctive, as well as a learning food gathering behavior. The nest huddlers (altricial) are fed by their parents. The food can be given in various ways. With most songbird species, the adults place the food directly into the open beaks of the nestlings. With storks and gulls, the collected food is regurgitated into the nest in front of the chicks. The young of pelicans and penguins reach into, respectively, the throat or crop of the parent. Hummingbirds place their beaks into those of their young and release the soft food pulp with pumping actions. Regurgitated food is mixed with digestive juices. The consistency of the pulp depends on the type of food, and the time it has been in the crop or stomach of the parent bird.

Open beaks, begging chirps, and the very conspicuous papillae in the corners of the mouths of the young of many bird species stimulate the feeding drive of the parents. If a chick is no longer hungry but continues to beg, it still gets some food offered, but if it doesn't immediately swallow it, the parent bird will retrieve it and give it to a more hun-

Black-throated Finch at nest.

gry chick. In this way, the food is equally divided among the young. In their turn, the chicks are stimulated to beg for food when they are aware of their parents' presence. They hear the parents flying in. The parents may utter gentle calls or crouch low over the nest (the vibrations activate the young into begging for food, which you can see for yourself: You need only gently scratch the side of the nest, and the young will immediately start begging for food). Ornithologists have studied the reactions of the young of various species. The wooden model of a gull's head was enough to get gull chicks begging for food. With woodpeckers, you only have to darken the nest entrance to get a similar result.

Frequency of Feeding

The frequency of feeding also depends on the particular species or on the type of food. If a large bird of prey, for example, catches a rabbit for its young, it will be enough for a few days. Smaller birds of prey may have to catch at least ten mice a day for their young. Tits have to work industriously all day to bring enough food for their young. The amount of food required by the chicks increases as they grow.

The feeding regimen can be seriously disturbed if one of the parent birds should die. The remaining parent will have to do all the feeding, working twice as hard. If the young don't get fed, for example, due to environmental factors, they will die after a certain time. Young swallows will live without food for a maximum of three weeks; during this time their body temperature will dramatically decrease. Most cage and aviary birds will not live without food longer than 24 to 48 hours.

Keeping the Nest Clean

Most wild birds keep their nests clean; but some don't! The parents remove the droppings of the young (which are conveniently enclosed in a tough membrane) and eat them, or take them away from the nest. By removing the droppings, the nest becomes less conspicuous to possible predators. Large birds of prey have no natural enemies and young deposit their droppings around the edge of the nest. Trogons, doves, motmots, kingfishers, and hoopoes don't practice nest hygiene.

Rate of Growth

The young of small species grow relatively faster in the nest than those of larger species. A day-old cuckoo hatchling, for example, weighs .07 ounce (2 g), but fully grown, at three weeks, it weighs 3.5 ounces (100 g). Some advanced nestlings can weigh more than their parents. This is at the time when they are about to gain independence and must seek their own food. As they are not initially expert at this, their added weight will stand them in good stead for the time being. The young of a Wilson's Petrel is, after 2 days, already able to maintain a constant body temperature; the Wren after 9 days and the Crag Martin, after 21 days. Nest huddlers grow faster than nest leavers. It is interesting to note that nest huddlers often have larger eyes, a heavier brain, and a larger alimentary canal.

The time that nest huddlers stay in the nest (juvenile stage) varies greatly among the species. In the case of most smaller songbird species, the time is two weeks at the most; larger songbirds, three weeks; doves, woodpeckers, bee-eaters, trogons, and hummingbirds, four weeks. Young Emperor Penguins are 35 to 39 weeks old before they join their parents in the water!

A knowledge of the habits and lifestyles of wild birds is a great help when it comes to incubating and rearing them artificially. We will discuss a few facts we need to know, in order to raise young birds into healthy adults.

Artificial Incubation: History

In the wild, it is clear that all kinds of factors can influence the success of the breeding season. For example, sudden cold spells, or heavy rains can result in breeding pairs abandoning their nests. And we can understand why! But with regard to the artificial brooding of eggs we should not think that everything runs itself. Of course, we know that in 4,000 years of artificial brooding we have taken some great steps forward. We find it quite normal when, in the spring, electrical incubators all over the world are helping to bring chicks of pheasants, quail, ducks, chickens, etc. into the world, but it is only 90 years since the first incubators appeared on the market. For various reasons, these incubators were strongly objected to, but it had been forgotten that artificial brooding has been performed for thousands of years (see page 40). Hieroglyphics in ancient Egyptian buildings, and the writings of such historical authors as Diadorus, Siculus, Plinius, von Moncony, Vessing, Rhevenot, Sicard, Granger, and Lucas have shown that domestic chicks were artificially brooded (e.g., without the help of "mother hen") in Egypt 4,000 years ago. At that time, the Egyptians had already developed some amazingly sophisticated techniques. Everyone knows that they built the pyramids, but did you know that they practiced all forms of the arts, and were even able to operate on the brain?

We can surely speculate that the discovery of artificial brooding arose as a result of the desire to increase the output of poultry; however, we don't know all the details.

Egyptian Methods

Particulars of the Egyptian incubation methods, i.e., measuring temperatures, raising humidity, and the success rate (50 to 70 percent should have been achieved) are now known, but at that time the procedures were kept strictly secret and only passed down from father to son. We know that the egg temperature was tested by holding the egg against the corner of the eye. Try it yourself and feel how temperature-sensitive this spot is. We also know that the breeders didn't use eggs that were more than a week old. Of course, candling lights were not known at the time but, by holding the egg up against the sunlight, they could check the age by the size of the air sac. Whether they could tell if an egg was fertile or infertile by this method, we don't know, but it is quite possible that they could.

The center for artificial incubation was in the village of Berme, Egypt, not far from Cairo. The breeders gathered eggs from throughout the land and brought them back to the village for incubating. According to Sicard, there were 386 incubation ovens that were used over a period of six months. Eight broods could be incubated in this period, thus a total of 3,088 broods. Réaumur calculated 30,000 chicks per brood and thus a total of 92,604,000 per breeding season.

The method of building the ovens could, of course, not be kept secret. The ovens certainly were not small, and we cannot help but wonder at the knowledge of this civilization. The incubation ovens consisted of a row of chambers connected by narrow openings that were easy to close off. More chambers above were also connected, and there were openings in the top for ventilation and light.

A mixture of chopped straw and manure was placed in the upper chambers. The smoke escaped through openings in the walls. The warmed air was conducted through vents into the brooding chambers and controlled by opening and closing them throughout the complex.

Eggs were continually being moved from chamber to chamber, because the temperature distribution was irregular. Hatchlings could be speedily dispatched to other areas with adequate rearing facilities.

Chinese Methods

We know less about the early Chinese methods of incubation, but we know that they had a knowledge of it at an early stage of their history. The Chinese incubated duck eggs. They were placed in layers, separated by felt paper, in barrellike containers. The containers were then placed in the heated canals of the incubation ovens. After 14 days,

the eggs were arranged in benches in a heated room and covered with cloth. The eggs were generally cooled and turned only once a day; only one record refers to "five times per day." The Chinese also tested the egg temperature against the corner of the eye.

Methods From Other Countries

We have no records of artificial incubation by the ancient Greeks or Romans, but much later the French physicist René-Antoine Ferchault de Réaumur (1683–1757) experimented in this area. In 1745, he had some success in brooding hens' eggs. Artificial incubation has been known in Europe for about 200 years, a short time when compared with the 4,000 years of the Egyptians and the Chinese! Réaumur himself was greatly helped by the use of his own invented, 80 degree thermometer (1 degree Réaumur = 5/4 degree C). At last we had a means of accurately measuring temperature. Today, all incubators are controlled by thermometer measurements, with the difference that we use the Celsius or Fahrenheit scales.

In Réaumur's incubators, many embryos were lost, due to the difficulty of maintaining constant temperatures and the correct humidity and ventilation. He covered his incubators with plaster for insulation.

The further development of incubators happened quickly. Sulzer built a steam-operated incubator in Berlin, Beguelin (1750) used a lamp as a heat source, and Champion (1770) used hot air. Bonnemain invented a hot-water incubator in Paris in 1780. He wanted to make a living out of his brooding but he failed because of the high losses of embryos. Too much emphasis was being placed on the maintenance of temperature, while omitting the other important factors of humidity and ventilation.

The Englishman Cantelo tried out another system in 1830. He used hot water flowing over glass or other waterproof material placed above the eggs. Seven years later, Baumayer devised a system whereby water, at a temperature of 104°F (40°C), was conducted through pipes lying over the eggs.

Around 1875, von Offele in Germany and Rouillier and Arnoult in France came up with a system using metal boxes that were filled with hot water every 12 hours. The eggs were arranged on a sloping surface beneath. Such water machines were used extensively for a time.

At the turn of the century, great progress was made when the control of humidity and ventilation was taken more seriously into account. Air-heated incubators came into being, using petroleum or electricity as a power source. The commercial aspects heightened considerably when the still-air incubators were replaced by box machines in which thousands of eggs could be brooded together. At last we had reached the standard the Egyptians had already reached 4,000 years ago!

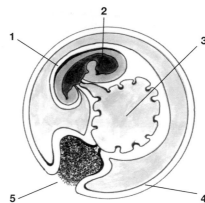

Development of the Embryo (#1)
1. *Fused chorion and allantois*
2. *Amnion*
3. *Yolk sac*
4. *Allantoic cavity*
5. *Remains of albumen*

Brooding in the Incubator

Artificial incubation of eggs has several important advantages:
- better hygiene (eggs are soiled in the nest);
- greater safety during the brooding process (no abandonment by the parents);
- less chance of eggs or young being infected by the adults;
- more control during hatching (being squashed or pecked to death by the parents or foster parents);
- more control of feeding when raising the young.

The incubator makes it all possible, and the closer we can get to natural development, the greater our successes will be.

Development of the Embryo

The satisfactory development of the embryo depends on the correct temperature, precise humidity, and

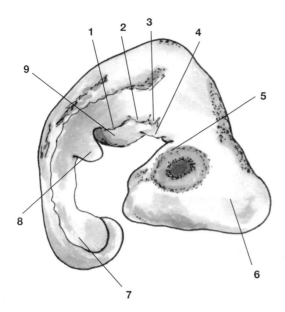

Development of the Embryo (#2)
1. to 3. Visceral arches, 4. Mandible, 5. Maxilla, 6. Mid-brain,
7. Limb bud, 8. Wing bud, 9. Heart

One- to four-day-old Black-throated Finches begging for food.

adequate ventilation. By taking these three parameters into consideration, the hobbyist will succeed in producing a living, fully developed hatchling—a wonder of nature!

The Correct Incubation Temperature

The lowest temperature required to start embryo development in an egg is about 82.4°F (28°C), but must be held constantly at 101.5°F (38.6°C) for all gallinaceous birds, or 98.5°F to 98.7°F (36.9–37.1°C) for the eggs of large parrots (*Eclectus*, macaws, and cockatoos, for example) or Australian parrots and parakeets, measured on the upper surface of the egg if using a still-air incubator, and 99.8°F (37.7°C) for gallinaceous birds, if using a motorized incubator.

Incubation Times

The incubation times in the incubator are the same as they are in the wild; it is very difficult to correctly speed up the natural process. By artificially increasing the correct incubation temperature, you will produce misformed chicks and, at 105°F (40.6°C), the embryos of chickens and many other bird species will die.

Incubation Thermometer

There are several makes of incubation thermometers on the market that can be used for monitoring the egg temperatures. Sometimes, such as during transport, a bump will cause the mercury column in the thermometer to separate. This can be fixed by placing the bulb of the thermometer in warm water so that the mercury rises and rejoins the separated parts. On cooling, the column should then stay in one piece.

Temperature Regulation

Thermostats

The warmth in the incubator is regulated with a thermostat that is set at the correct temperature for brooding.

Ether-Capsule Thermostats

These are used in many incubators. They consist of two or more round, flat, copper capsules, filled with ether and hermetically sealed. They work as follows: The capsules can be screwed closer to or further from a built-in microswitch by means of a threaded rod. When the switch is pressed in, the heating elements are turned off, and when the pressure is released, they come on again.

Ether has a property that makes it expand and contract with the slightest temperature variations. Thus, when the temperature goes too high, the capsules expand and press off the power; then, as the temperature decreases, the capsules contract and switch on the heating elements again.

By setting the ether capsules at the correct distance from the switch, we can thus maintain the constant required temperature in the incubator.

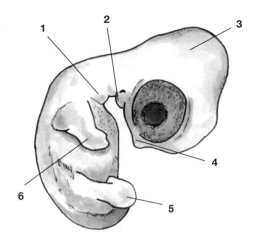

Development of the Embryo (#3)
1. Visceral arch, 2. Mandible, 3. Mid-brain, 4. Maxilla
5. Toe plate, 6. Digital plate

The correct use of the ether capsule is important for a good hatching result and the aviculturist must take good care of it; an efficiently working ether capsule should expand by about 0.16 inch (4 mm) after a few minutes of heating.

It is advisable to keep a few reserve capsules in readiness, in case of failures due to material stress. Old, badly insulated incubators are particularly hard on the capsules which will quickly deteriorate from overwork.

There is another disadvantage of the ether capsules: They are also affected by air pressure (due to sudden barometric changes, for example) so should be monitored at regular intervals during changeable weather.

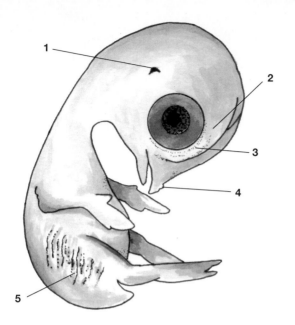

Development of the Embryo (#4):
1. External auditory opening, 2. Eye lid, 3. Nictitating
membrane, 4. Egg tooth, 5. Feather germs

Oil-filled and Electronic Thermostats

Some incubators are fitted with thermostats that are not affected by barometric pressure. Such thermostats are equipped with rather expensive, sensitive, and delicate, oil-filled "feelers." The biggest advantage of these thermostats is that they don't have to be reset each time there's a weather change! Oil-filled thermostats are, however, not suitable for still-air incubators, which react too slowly.

The whole thermostat and the "feeler" are available separately because the "feeler" is so delicate.

Electronic thermostats are now also available, in which the temperature and even the turning of the eggs is all done electronically.

Precise Humidity Control

In addition to the correct temperature, precise air humidity in the incubator and in the room where it is installed is of utmost importance. Those amateur aviculturists who underestimate the importance of humidity during incubation will experience poor results as dry air will lead to dead embryos. During the incubation process, each egg must lose a certain amount of moisture, so that the air sac expands. At the end of the incubation cycle, an egg will have lost between 13 and 15 percent of its weight. The loss of moisture from the egg is a gradual process and should not take place during initial storage of the egg; otherwise, it will already be too dry for embryo development to progress satisfactorily.

Humidity Control in the Incubator

The relative humidity in the incubator should be maintained at about 50 percent during incubation and increased to 65 to 70 percent during hatching, for gallinaceous birds and waterfowl. Parrots require about 45 percent relative humidity at hatching time.

The humidity can be measured with a wet-bulb hygrometer. This consists of a column of mercury in a glass tube marked from 40 to 100 percent and a wick about 2.8 inches (7 cm) in length, which is attached with a fine wire to the mercury bulb. The base of the wick is immersed in a waterbath (use boiled and recooled water or distilled water). The hygrometer will work only at temperatures between 99.5 and 100.4°C (37.5–38°C). Deteriorating or calcified wicks must be replaced. You can obtain a wet-bulb hygrometer and spare wicks from your supplier.

The round, dry thermometer is perhaps easier to use. It only needs to be wrapped in a wet cloth for an hour every couple of months. The reading should then be 95 to 98 percent. If this is not the case, it can be readjusted before use. These may be used in small still-air incubators (see page 72).

Humidity Control in the Incubation Room and in the Egg Storage Room

Humidity in the incubator arises from regularly topped-up, water-filled trays placed in the incubator base.

A relative humidity of 55 percent in the incubation room is about right. Too great a difference in relative humidity inside and outside the incubator can be harmful to the incubating eggs. The relative humidity in the brooding room is monitored with a hygrometer that also shows the temperature. Humidity can be maintained by using water trays or misters.

The relative humidity in the egg storage room is best maintained

One-day-old Plum-headed Finches (see also page 16).

around 75 percent as eggs must not lose too much moisture prior to being incubated. Many beginners lose valuable eggs because they don't take this into consideration. A hygrometer/thermometer can also be used here to monitor humidity and temperature (about 59°F [15°C]). Several water trays will provide the necessary moisture.

Adequate Ventilation

Developing embryos produce carbon dioxide and therefore require a constant supply of oxygen-rich fresh air. It is thus essential to ventilate the incubator by regulating the vents. The instructions supplied with the various incubator models will give you concise directions for operating the vents.

Placing Eggs in the Incubator

When you are ready to incubate stored eggs, you must take adequate care. Before putting them in the warm incubator, they should first be placed in the incubator room

Incubator.

Brooding with the Still-Air Incubator

The still-air incubator operates similarly to natural brooding because the heat source is above the eggs and consists of a series of long-life bulbs that are very economical to use.

The still-air incubator has no ventilator, but the warm air circulates slowly through it. The difference in temperature between the upper and lower surfaces of the eggs is optimal and similar to that in natural brooding.

Not so long ago, I heard the following statement: "The broody hen is perhaps easier, but the incubator is more interesting and educational!" It's up to you to decide if this quotation is correct.

so that their temperature is slowly raised from the storage temperature of 59 to 77°F (15–25°C). This will take about an hour, after which you can place the eggs in the incubator that is set at incubation temperature. Tests have shown that too sudden temperature increases are bad for the embryos!

Where to Place the Still-Air Incubator

Taking ventilation and the supply of fresh air into consideration, the still-air incubator should be placed in a room maintained at 50°F (10°C). During incubation, fresh air is perhaps more important than you may think. Baking and cooking fumes, smoke, or a stale atmosphere are not favorable to the incubation process. The machine is best placed in an isolated spot on a level shelf, preferably at eye level. Direct sunlight is fatal to embryos; *never* place your incubator in sunlight!

Incubating the Eggs

At least 24 hours before placing your sorted eggs into the incubator, the machine must be warmed up

Incubator.

and set at the correct brooding temperature. The incubation thermometer, usually a mercury thermometer with an easily readable scale, is placed in the middle of the egg layer. It must be placed accurately, the bulb at the same level as the upper surface of an egg.

The incubation hygrometer is also placed in the egg layer, with the wick placed in the filled waterbath. Do not leave the inspection lamp on; this is only used to inspect the eggs during incubation. If you leave the lamp on, the temperature and air circulation can be adversely affected. The air vents must be set as recommended for the incubator model.

When you set the incubation temperature, the heating elements should switch off automatically when the desired temperature is reached, and on again as it decreases. If this does not happen precisely, you will have to repair or replace the thermostat. The ether capsule (see page 69), in particular, is very sensitive and you are advised to stock a few spares in case of malfunction.

If the relative humidity rises too much, it will be necessary to adjust the incubator vents until the correct percentage is achieved. If the relative humidity is too low, you should spray the interior of the incubator with a fine-mist sprayer, and be sure that the water trays are constantly topped off.

When the machine has worked fault-free, and the set temperature and humidity has remained constant for 12 to 24 hours, you can

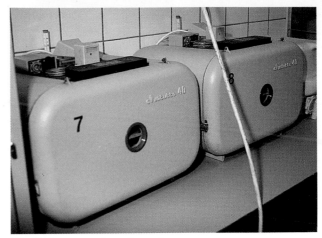

Incubators come in various sizes.

place the eggs in the incubator. Twelve hours later, the eggs will be warmed through.

Egg Turning

Incubating eggs must be turned at least three times a day. This is necessary because the embryo, in the lighter yolk, floats toward the upper

Incubator for large eggs.

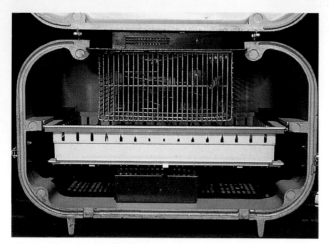
The inside of an incubator.

surface and could adhere to the membrane, causing malformation and death of the developing chick. Turning also encourages movement in the embryo that is favorable for growth.

The eggs should not be turned completely over (180 degrees); a quarter-turn is adequate. When you turn the eggs, place those on the outside of the layer into the center, and vice versa, so that irregular incubation is avoided. Starting three days before hatching is expected, the eggs should not be turned; the chicks must have the opportunity to gain a favorable position for hatching; otherwise, the chicks may start to pip at the wrong part of the egg, with the chance that they will get their beaks gummed up with albumen and suffocate. Therefore, eggs are turned regularly throughout incubation except for the last three days.

Ventilating and Cooling the Incubator

Good ventilation and supply of fresh air in the incubator is of extreme importance for the developing embryos. At first, the oxygen requirement is relatively small, but this increases during incubation and reaches its high point just before hatching when the chick begins to use its lungs to respire. The embryo absorbs oxygen and releases carbon dioxide. Fresh air contains 21 percent oxygen and you must ensure that this percentage is maintained in the incubator by ventilating it daily. As a rule, you should ventilate and cool *for one minute* for each day the incubation period has progressed, which in many cases will mean for twenty minutes at the end of the incubation time.

The Incubating Temperature in the Still-Air Incubator

Warmth influences the development of the embryo; however, the temperature must not be too high or too low. Research into incubating temperatures of pheasants, turkeys, and chickens has shown that the incubating temperature of eggs is not constant; slight rises, and greater decreases in temperature occur. From this we can conclude that higher temperatures are more dangerous than lower ones. The eggs of pheasants are more susceptible to high temperatures than those of chickens. For all gallinaceous birds' eggs, the temperature of the incubator should be set at 101.3°F (38.5°C), at the upper surface of the eggs. A very small variation is acceptable, but bear in mind that the embryo *will* die at a temperature of 104°F (40°C) or higher; see also page 68. The recommended temperature must be maintained throughout the incubation period except for the turning and cooling sessions.

Humidity Control in the Still-Air Incubator

There is little air circulation in the still-air incubator so the relative humidity must not be too high, or the eggs won't lose enough moisture. A relative humidity of 55 percent is thus adequate in this kind of incubator, from the first day, until two days before hatching, when it should be increased to 65 percent. Moreover, during the last four days, you should sprinkle water, warmed to 104°F (40°C), over the eggs. During the whole incubation period, each egg (for example, that of a pheasant) should lose 0.17 to 0.26 grams (.006–.009 ounce) in weight per day, due to moisture loss. When hatching begins, all vents should be open to allow adequate fresh air into the machine.

Interruption of the Incubating Process

Should there be an electrical power failure or drop, do not keep opening the incubator lid to read the temperature. Development of the embryo will slow down somewhat, and, as long as this is no more than 8 to 10 hours, it will do no harm; the eggs will hatch a little later. You

Thermo-hygrometer.

may occasionally forget to replace an egg in the incubator. If the room temperature is not too low, and you replace the egg as soon as you discover it, this shouldn't cause too much damage.

Eggs with Various Hatching Times

In the height of the season (May), the incubator is usually full of eggs and the breeder must try to get them all to hatch around the same time. Why? The body temperature of chicks about to hatch can unfavorably influence the development of embryos at a younger stage, if the respective eggshells are close together. In addition, the movement and cheeping of an advanced embryo can influence a younger one to hatch before time, often before the yolk sac is fully absorbed—a dangerous situation!

Infertile eggs must also be removed as soon as possible. It has

Egg scale.

been found that chicks hatching from eggs around an infertile egg are often weak, or even die in the shell. This is a puzzle that has yet to be scientifically solved, but this phenomenon has been known for a long time in commercial hatcheries.

The efficient aviculturist will have a separate hatching incubator in which the relative humidity is maintained at 65 percent throughout the

season, and in which the eggs are placed at hatching time.

If you let the eggs hatch in the brooding incubator, you will have all types of shell pieces, feathers, skin pieces, and so on that can pose a threat of infection. Moreover, the necessary increase in humidity at hatching time will be unfavorable for those embryos that are not so far advanced.

The Chicks Are Hatched

The newly hatched chicks are left in the incubator until they are quite dry. Then they are taken to the rearing room where the temperature is maintained at 86 to 95°F (30–35°C) by using a suspended heat lamp (60-100-150-200 watt) with or without a reflector.

Maintenance and Disinfection of the Still-Air Incubator

After each incubation cycle, you should clean out your incubator with a vacuum cleaner before disinfecting all parts of the machine with, for example, Novassan or Lysol.

Still-Air Incubators with a Fan

The still-air incubators available on the market that are equipped with a small ventilating fan (alleged to promote even distribution of warm air) are useless machines. You have either a still-air ventilator, or a motorized incubator—it's neither one thing nor another! First of

Incubator with quail eggs.

all, the fan does not have the power to distribute the air evenly and you will end up with temperature variations as much as five degrees and all the problems that arise from it. Second, such machines don't have a hatching tray, and the close-to-hatching eggs are exposed to an air stream that is much too strong, especially for pheasant eggs.

Brooding with the Motorized Incubator

Motorized incubators presently available have fully automatic egg turning devices that turn the eggs 90 degrees, 24 times a day. They are mainly used for incubating the eggs of gallinaceous birds and waterfowl. The most modern machines for the hobbyist are equipped with the newest devices.

The advantages of a motorized incubator are:
- You can continue to place eggs in it until all egg trays are filled.
- The machine is labor-saving because the eggs are turned by a fully automatic motor.
- The eggs do not need to be cooled throughout the brooding period and the ventilation is easy to control.

Where to Place the Motorized Incubator

Like the still-air incubator, the motorized incubator should be situated in a room with constant temperature and humidity. The machine is placed on a firm, solid surface at a height of about 28 inches (71 cm). It should be vibration-free—vibrations can be fatal to developing embryos. The machine should not be placed against a wall, as this will increase vibration and noise, even with the most modern, quiet machines.

Before Starting the Motor

Before the motor is used, you should check that all the egg trays are firmly affixed in position, and that the moving parts can move freely. Next, fill the water tray with distilled water or rainwater.

The reservoir on the hygrometer is filled with distilled water, and the wick should be clean and new. (Spare wicks can be bought!) After plugging the machine into a power point, switch it on, and you should hear a soft humming noise and see the motor turning. After setting the thermostat control, the required temperature should be reached in about one hour. The machine should be switched on, tested, and adjusted for 24 hours before eggs are placed in it.

The Correct Incubating Temperature

The incubating temperature is adjusted with a control knob; turn it left to increase temperature, right to decrease it.

Incubators fitted with ether-capsule thermostats must be re-adjusted with barometric pressure

Table 5
Incubating Temperatures

Species	Temperature
Chickens, bantams, jungle fowl	99.5 to 99.8°F (37.5–37.7°C)
Pheasants, guineafowl, peafowl, partridges, and quail	98.2 to 98.6°F (36.8–37.0°C)
Waterfowl	98.2 to 98.4°F (36.8–36.9°C)

changes. Those fitted with electronic thermostats should not need to be adjusted.

The incubating temperature inside the incubator is always 1 to 1.5°F higher than that measured on the glass.

Young lovebirds in a plastic strawberry basket lined with facial tissue. It is recommended that during the first 5 to 6 days of life, the chicks should be placed in the brooder in separate containers.

Loading the Eggs

After ensuring that the machine is working and set properly, the fresh (two to ten days old) eggs are taken from the storeroom and held for an hour at incubator room temperature before being arranged in the incubator trays. They usually are arranged with the pointed end downward.

Each egg tray is provided with removable and rearrangeable strips so that eggs of various sizes can be arranged without them rolling around. Any parts not filled with eggs should be filled with balls of paper or foam rubber; the eggs must be "fixed" so they cannot roll around.

To prevent overcrowding in the hatching tray, it is advisable to load only to one-third capacity and to make up the rest at three-day intervals. Eggs are only loaded when the trays are horizontal. Don't forget to turn on the motor after loading the eggs.

Inspecting the Incubating Eggs

During the incubation period, the eggs are inspected twice, with a special candler that has a built-in mirror (available from your supplier). This is best done in the dark.

After the sixth day, fertile eggs will, in most cases, show the developing embryo as a red patch surrounded by tiny blood vessels. Infertile eggs will be clear.

On the eighteenth day, fertile eggs will be completely dark, except for the air chamber at the blunt end of the egg. Infertile eggs and those with a dead embryo are removed as soon as possible and discarded. Infertile eggs, of waterfowl, in particular, give off foul-smelling gases that will pollute the fresh air in the incubator.

After each inspection, the motor must be turned on again. The motor should also continue working until the last chick has hatched.

Disinfecting the Machine

Motorized incubators must also be disinfected after each brood and not only at the end of the season. Use Lysol (see page 50), which does not attack or corrode metal or timber, but kills all germs.

Relative Humidity in the Motorized Incubator

The relative humidity in the motorized incubator is kept at about 50 to 55 percent during the entire incubation period, except for the last day of incubation and hatching day when it should be raised to 65 percent, or 75 percent for waterfowl. The color of the egg membrane will tell you if you have incubated at too low or too high humidity. If it is pure white and dry, the humidity is too low; if it is grayish white and moist, the chicks will not dry out at hatching. If water runs out of the machine, that means disaster—the humidity is much too high! Once the eggs are hatched, the relative humidity should be brought back to 50 percent as soon as possible, and the water tray should be removed.

Young Black-headed Caiques ready to be fed.

It may be necessary to use a fine-mist sprayer to increase humidity the day before and during hatching. Spray only in the hatching tray and *never* near the thermometer sensor. A damp sensor, oil or electronic, will give a false temperature reading. If damp, it should be carefully dried with a dry cloth. Remember that the less often you open the machine, the better it will hold its humidity!

Ventilation in the Motorized Incubator

The incubator must be ventilated in such a way as to not affect the relative humidity. Correct ventilation is a question of feeling and experience. Only slight ventilation is generally required, especially if the lid is opened occasionally to add or inspect eggs.

During hatching, the ventilation can be increased, especially if the hatchlings start to pant! The slow

Containers to keep the youngsters warm.

Too Much Ventilation Is Dangerous

In the motorized incubator, the ventilating fan, turned fully on, will turn at about 1,200 revolutions per minute, depending on the motor of the unit. The fan ensures an even distribution of the warm air over the eggs. If overventilated, you will get the same effect as drying laundry in the wind! The eggs will lose too much moisture and the membranes will become hard and tough. The carbon dioxide waste will not be able to escape and oxygen will not be absorbed. The eggshells of pheasants, in particular, are so porous that they can hardly stand a whirling air current. The hatching tray must therefore be almost entirely closed at hatching time.

increase in size of the air chamber in the egg gives the best indication that all is going well.

Table 6
Relative Humidity

Bird Species	During Incubation		During Hatching	
	Degrees (wet bulb)	*Percent relative humidity*	*Degrees*	*Percent relative humidity*
Chickens, bantams and jungle fowl	82 to 85°F (27.8–29.4°C)	48–54	90°F (32.2°C)	68
Pheasants, guinea fowl, peafowl, partridges, and quail	86°F (30°C)	55	90°F (32.2°C)	68
All waterfowl	86°F (30°C)	55	91°F (32.8°C)	70

Temperature and Aviculture: an Overview

For successful artificial incubation, it is first advisable to look at what happens during the breeding season in the wild. In nature, things such as sudden cold spells or heavy rains can affect brooding in a particular area, leading to abandonment of nest, eggs, or young.

In our aviaries and breeding rooms, young parrots, finches, and similar-sized species develop best at a constant temperature and humidity and a 10-hour photoperiod. In outdoor aviaries, it seems that young birds of the same species raised in the spring do better than those raised later in the year. This also occurs among various species in the wild.

We have arrived at a recommended temperature of 98.6°F (37°C) for newly hatched young. This temperature can be maintained for two to six hours after hatching, or longer if it seems necessary. After this time, the down (if there is any present) should be dry and the young fully active. As soon as the young look dry and are active, you can drop the temperature in the brooder one degree (97.6°F [36.4°C] appears to be more than adequate) for four to five days. After this period, the temperature is reduced to 95°F (35°C) and held for seven to ten days before reducing it to 93°F (33.9°C). When down feathers are beginning to develop, giving the chick a protective coat, the temperature is reduced to 85°F (29.4°C) then, after another couple of days, to room temperature (78 to 83°F [25.6–28.3°C]), but only if the chicks are well feathered.

Whatever the species, the temperature is adjusted up or down, unless the chicks show signs of discomfort. You will soon see if the young are uncomfortable; at too high a temperature they will gape and pant, at too low a temperature they will cheep and huddle together for warmth. It is important to realize that single chicks require more warmth than a group.

Research has shown that naturally hatched chicks (by parents or foster parents) removed for hand-rearing have a lower temperature requirement than incubator-hatched chicks—and that is not so amazing! In the wild, the parents cannot feed and brood the young like clockwork; moreover, the temperature outside the nest will vary from day to day, even lower at night. In other words, the young are strongly dependent on each other for warmth. There is no constant temperature to speak of, nor a constant supply of food. When the chicks are cold, the food intake is lower, as digestion takes longer because the chick is less active. It is therefore understandable that such youngsters are better adapted to temperature variations. Chicks removed for hand-rearing (after a week or more) can thus be kept at a lower temperature, unless they are removed during hot weather and it is cooler in the nursery.

Try to "copy" the outdoor temperature as much as possible, but if this is higher than that stated above, reduce it over four to five days.

My Tip: You can easily check the temperature of an unfeathered chick: Hold the tip of its wing against the corner of your eye or between your lips. If the wingtip feels really cold, the temperature in the brooder is too low and should be adjusted. This works only with a solitary chick; more chicks together keep each other warm by huddling together. This method also will not work if the chick is feathered and you cannot contact the naked skin (a good indication as to how well feathers insulate).

If chicks huddle together in the brooder, they are too cold. You can see this among naked, as well as feathered, chicks. If the chicks are comfortable, there is minimum body contact. You can see this in wild birds sitting together on a twig: if it is cold, they will huddle together; if it is warm, they sit separately.

Humidity and Aviculture: an Overview

As a rule of thumb, we can say that a minimum of 40 percent relative humidity should be maintained in the nursery. Various makes of commercial humidifiers are available. We know ourselves that dry air is not good for our skin; it becomes dry and flaky. The same goes for our birds that already have a naturally dry skin. Moreover, too low a humidity promotes slow feather growth (and too high a humidity promotes premature feather growth, which frequently causes a delay in body growth). We must also be aware that high temperature plus high humidity promotes prolific fungal growth, which may endanger the health of our birds.

Lighting

Light in general is extremely important in the life of man and animals. For example, it influences the reproductive activities of birds. In the temperate zones it is the increase in daylight duration (photoperiod) that influences the breeding cycle to begin. Due to differences in day length, the same species of bird breed later in upstate New York than they do in Florida. In the tropics, where the days are more or less the same length throughout the year, the breeding cycle is influenced by availability of food. For example, Australian Grass Finches begin to breed after the rains, when enough food (such as grass seed) is available to raise their young.

Cage and aviary birds are also influenced by photoperiod. I have tried various experiments in this field—by gradual increase over a number of days, the number of hours of light were increased to 15. It became clear that more than 14 hours of light had hardly any influence on the breeding condition of my birds. With less than eight hours of daylight, the birds had too little time to feed adequately. I now try to give all my birds a minimum of ten hours light per day, whether they are in garden aviaries, breeding cages in the bird room, or the nursery. The birds in the nursery have a subdued light after feeding. It is, however, never completely dark, even at night. At nighttime, various night lamps are left on so that the birds can always see what is going on around them; thus, panic and stress are avoided. Fluorescent fixtures are best for use in the nursery, as they give adequate light to work by.

Substrate (Bedding)

For as long as I can remember, I have used thin, dust-free pine shavings for my brooding containers, and facial tissue for hatchlings. Paper towels and similar materials are frequently rough, with the chance of paper cuts, especially with regard to the toes and feet of very young baby birds. Don't use shiny "slippery" paper (wax paper, for example), which can cause splayed legs.

Recycled paper or grass pellets are available on the market. Both are highly absorbent, but make it difficult for young birds of various sorts to walk, especially if it is more than 1 inch (2.5 cm) deep.

I am less enthusiastic about ground corncob as bedding, after several times seeing stressed birds peck it up. This can cause obstruction and other problems.

Many fanciers use kitchen towels, old bath towels, and such but I don't particularly recommend them. Birds are soon sitting in their own droppings, and the loops in the cloth are dangerous for nails and toes.

Although cedar bedding is quite popular as a substrate, there is a drawback to using it. Where ventilation is bad, cedar bedding will cause eye irritation and breathing problems (used in closed rooms for gerbils, mice, and guinea pigs, for example, it causes hair loss as well as the two problems mentioned). Always use nontoxic beddings!

Types of Brooder Containers

Containers must, of course, never be too small. Bear in mind that, as young birds grow and feather up, they will need adequate space to avoid walking all over each other. Such behavior can be stressful and even cause loss of appetite. Imagine a young macaw that stands up and beats its wings (which it frequently does) while its companions around it try to avoid being struck! A number of half-grown macaws in a strawberry basket won't be very comfortable.

Let's look at a few options for brooder containers:

Human baby incubators and intensive care units are frequently used by veterinarians as well as by experienced aviculturists. The big advantage of such units is that the temperature can easily be controlled, whatever the circumstances. They are not always easy to clean.

Old fish aquariums are frequently used. The baby birds are placed on a heating pad with a thick towel (no loops!) wrapped around it. Use a heating pad that is smaller than the aquarium base, so that the area around it is unheated. This will allow the birds to sit in a cooler spot if they should feel too warm. Always ensure that the young cannot come into direct contact with the glass or metal floor of the aquarium; the aquarium base can overheat if a heating pad is incorrectly set, causing the possibility of burned breasts or feet. Aquariums can also be difficult to adequately clean and disinfect. If you use several aquariums, it is best to block the view between them with sheets of cardboard so that the clutches of birds cannot see each other. According to many aviculturists, this avoids stress—a point with which I wholeheartedly agree.

Commercial baby brooders are available in many types and prices. I am not aware of any that have a filtration system. The less expensive models are made from plastic or even styrofoam. Due to their simple construction, most models are not safe from airborne contaminents, and are also difficult to keep clean. Even the heat source (frequently just a simple light bulb) is not always reliable—think what would happen in the event of a power failure. Fortunately, there are plastic or plexiglass models that are heated by warm water. The water, contained in a tank, is heated with an aquarium heater and thermostat, set at the required temperature. Even with a power failure, the water takes a while to lose its heat—in my view, a calming thought. One possible disadvantage is that the air circulation in the chamber is limited, meaning that a high humidity will prevail. Also, I find these models difficult to clean.

My tip: The simplest brooders have frequent heating problems. Many aviculturists use light bulbs or the above-mentioned heating pads. I know some hobbyists who use space heaters to heat the whole nursery, including the brooding containers, maintaining the temperature at about 85°F (29.4°C). Bulbs and heating pads can pose dangers. For example, a number of clip-on lamps may be used around the top of an "aquarium brooder." Be sure that a lamp cannot fall into the tank; think of the damage that could do! Do not place lamps too close to baby birds. Test with your hand or with a thermometer. The temperature for most of our birds should be, as we already know (see page 81), 98.6°F (37°C) for hatchlings; 97.6°F (36.4°C) for chicks up to five days old; 95°F (35°C) for chicks up to nine or ten days old, and 93°F (33.9°C) for chicks ten days old to adequate feathering. Once the young are adequately feathered, then 85°F (29.4°C) is a suitable temperature for most chicks. I would also recommend not using clear or white bulbs, but colored (amber) ones. These are gentler on the eyes of birds (as well as aviculturists), and prevent stress. Obviously, bulbs should be changed regularly, before they expire. The expected life of a bulb is usually indicated on its package. Make a note of the date you start to use it.

Warning: Heating pads can be very dangerous to baby birds as they cannot be thermostatically controlled. Get to know the workings of the various heating pads available on the market, discuss with colleagues the various advantages and disadvantages, and follow the manufacturer's instructions implicitly, in order to avoid the possibility of overheating the birds. As stated above, make sure the bird can step off the heat source if it gets too warm!

Paper bags and cardboard boxes are often used by experienced breeders. The familiar brown bags are always available and can be easily disposed of and replaced when soiled. Fill the bottom of the bag with a few handfuls of bedding (see page 83). Of course, there is no heating, and these bags are often used only in heated nurseries. Once the young are too large for a bag, they can be transferred to a cardboard box. A suspended reflector lamp can be used for warmth. The boxes must be regularly replaced as they become soiled with food spillings and droppings. A substrate is strongly recommended. Many breeders place older youngsters on a wire bottom, with absorbent bedding beneath.

Plastic containers, such as strawberry baskets, margarine containers, flower pots, etc. are frequently used because they are inexpensive and easy to clean. A wire bottom with absorbent bedding is recommended. Jordan correctly recommends square or rectangular containers, as there seems to be a correlation between round containers and crooked beaks, especially in large birds like macaws and cockatoos.[1]

Chicks and Their Care and Management

The first day, after hatching, I place each chick in a separate container—depending on the size of the chick, this may be a rectangular strawberry box or margarine container. With this method I can inspect each youngster at any time of the day and study the droppings of the individual bird. As bedding I use soft tissue paper such as facial tissue. The young from a particular clutch are placed in one temperature-controlled brooder.

[1]Rick Jordan, *Parrot Incubation Procedures* (Ontario: Silvio Mattacchione and Co., 1989).

Young Maroon-bellied Conure testing a piece of cake.

The temperature is maintained at 98.6°F (37°C) for the first six hours, then reduced to 97.6°F (36.4°C) for five days.

After five days I place the young from a clutch together in a larger container. There is no reason not to place chicks of similar age, even of other species, together, as long as they are fit and healthy. Chicks seem to enjoy being together, as long as there is enough space. Sick chicks must, of course, be isolated from the other birds.

Once the birds have developed adequate feathering (most of the pin feathers "unrolled" and adequate feathering on head and breast), they will tolerate room temperature if introduced to it gradually. By now they will be starting to beat their wings and will eat more, though their weight will decrease. Be sure that they are fed regularly.

They may begin to peck at the substrate and, although they may be well fed, they may start to eat it. In such cases, it is best to place them on a raised wire bottom, so that they cannot eat bedding, droppings, or food waste. At this time, many aviculturists switch from spoon to syringe, especially for large birds such as macaws and cockatoos. When the weaning period is imminent, more solid food is introduced into the diet.

When the birds are more or less fully feathered, they can be placed in separate cages. I prefer cages with a gauze or wire bottom so that the birds don't sit in their own feces, and so that spilled food is out of reach. If the bars of the cage bottom are set too far apart (with the danger that the birds could get their feet trapped), place a grill or a piece of aviary wire over them. Be sure that there are no sharp points in the mesh, which could cause injuries. Corncob bedding (the birds cannot eat it; see page 83) or pine shavings are adequate for use in the base of such cages.

When the chicks are ready to be weaned, they will require deeper and larger food and water vessels. The birds should lose little weight at this time, and if you have kept weight graphs, which I recommend (see page 113), you will see that the growth curve will stop descending and flatten out into a plateau. After a few days, the curve can start to go down again. As long as the bird is fit and healthy, this should cause no concern; a slight loss of weight at fledging time is inevitable.

You will notice that the birds will become more restive and will begin to refuse hand-feeding. If you allow it, they may play with the feeding spoon but will hardly take any food from it. Now is the time to give the birds a variety of foods to sample themselves. Millet spray, soaked seeds (sunflower for large birds, canary grass seeds, millet and rape seeds for smaller species—though larger bird species like small seeds too), mung beans, and other pulses can be offered, in addition to the rearing food that they are used to, which should be gradually reduced. The weaning process is discussed in greater detail on page 113.

Never stop giving rearing food "overnight"—this could disturb the delicate bacterial balance in your birds' digestive system. The weaning process should be a gradual affair

A hungry Blue-fronted Amazon. At this moment there are, among others, pied yellow, blue and lutino mutations.

and the first solid foods offered should be easily digestible. Try to spill as little food as possible during feeding and, after each feed, clean up the birds with lukewarm water. In order to prevent the birds from becoming saturated and chilled, use a clip-on lamp or something similar for drying.

Chapter Five
Proper Avian Nutrition

Introduction

The expression "So many men, so many minds" can be applied to formulas for baby birds. Even commercial hand-feeding diets are given as one pleases. Nutritionist T. Roudybush and his colleagues, for example, declared in the 1980s that optimal growth occurred in hand-fed baby cockatiels that were given a diet containing 20 percent protein. With protein levels above 20 percent, however, growth was depressed and chicks began to show behavioral abnormalities.

The author of this book and his coworkers at the University of Utrecht (The Netherlands) have shown that wild birds, as well as cage and aviary birds, require an average of 17 percent protein in the diet.

At the present time, "pet bird nutrition" is receiving much attention, especially in Europe where aviculture has been practiced for several centuries. In the United States, where the data from the poultry industry were once the only guidelines for commercial bird food manufacturers, much attention had also been turned to pet bird nutrition in recent times. Aviculturists work from day to day with various bird species, from canary to African Gray Parrot, from Wood Duck to Golden Pheasant. I believe that the more we bird breeders know about what species eat in the wild, and try to reproduce this diet as closely as possible for our captive birds, we will be a long way up the right road!

"Poly-unsaturates aside," say John and Pat Stoodley in their book *Genus Amazona*, "many of these glossy, round-looking parrots suffer heart conditions and their breeding records are poor." And, indeed, the disadvantage of many parrot seed mixtures is that they have a very high percentage of sunflower seeds. As parrots in general have a very good sense of taste, and sunflower seeds taste sweet, it is obvious that parrots will prefer them. Many hookbeaks, given the chance, will eventually eat nothing but sunflower seeds. This one-sided diet is very unhealthy for the birds and, in many, apart from getting too fat (especially if kept in a cage), their plumage deteriorates because *lysine*, a protein essential for feather growth, is deficient in the diet. Moreover, ironic as it may seem, sunflowers do not grow in the natural habitats of these parrots!

Many breeders are skeptical that commercial hand-feeding diets are incomplete and not nearly as good as their "homemade" mixtures of monkey biscuits, peanut butter, and human baby formula! As far as I can make out, in most cases the truth lies somewhere between the two extremes. I believe, indeed, that the commercial formulas are not complete. The addition of various foodstuffs to commercial hand-rearing formulas should provide a balanced diet for various species, providing we give them the types of food they would eat in the wild. By meeting with members of bird clubs and veterinarians, we can soon find out what particular bird species need in their diet, though we must be prepared to listen to the various opinions. Don't be afraid to speak to fellow aviculturists—listen to what they have to say, and read as much as possible about the bird species you want to raise. Read the ingredients and directions on the labels of the packs of commercial hand-feeding diets and consult your veterinarian if you are not clear about them. Many manufacturers also give an 800 number so that you can phone for free advice. And be sure that your chosen diet is not too low in fat (minimum 10 percent, maximum 15 percent) if you, for example, want to raise macaws and conures (to prevent stunting of growth). Check also the ratio of calcium to phosphorus, the level of vitamin D_3 (in IU per pound or kilogram), and the levels of protein and fiber. An excellent book

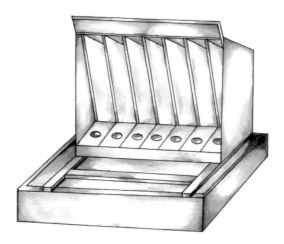

Seed feeder that allows seeds to be offered separately.

for such information is *Feeding Your Pet Bird* by Petra M. Burgmann, D.V.M., Barron's, 1993.

Unfortunately, many birdlovers believe that it is easy to hand-rear baby birds— "once the young have hatched, put them in a brooder at the correct temperature and feed regularly with a diet from the petshop, after bringing it to the right temperature." An easy task, they imply!

Well, it's certainly not quite that simple! The choice of a particular formula is naturally a matter of personal preference, but should always be taken with a big dose of hands-on experience, whether yours or somebody else's.

Food Quality

We cannot dispute that food quality is essential but there is another aspect that the breeder

Seed feeder for mixed seeds or pellets.

must constantly take into consideration. Whether we use our own baby-bird formula, or a commercial formula, there is always the danger of microbial contamination. There are three kinds of food-borne bacteria:

1. bacteria that multiply in the intestinal tract and cause infection in the host, e.g., *Salmonella*;
2. bacteria that grow and liberate toxins into food before it is eaten by the birds, e.g., botulinal and staphylococcal food poisoning; and
3. bacteria that apparently act through a dual mechanism, e.g., *Clostridium perfringens*, *C. colinum*, and *Escheridia coli*.

Colibacterial Infections

Colibacillosis is, for example, caused by *E. coli* (see also page 132). Colibacterial infections mostly manifest themselves in intestinal dis-

turbances as a result of toxin release. Quail, and to a lesser extent, chickens, pheasants, grouse, and young pigeons can be affected by *Clostridium colinum*, which causes similar intestinal disturbances. These are the so-called anerobic bacteria, which means that they can survive without oxygen. The waste products of these bacteria poison the intestinal walls, resulting in destruction of the lining so that food can no longer be absorbed into the bloodstream. The liver and spleen can also be affected.

Of course, there are other microorganisms that can contaminate food. What we have discussed above is sufficient for our purpose here, but anyone wishing to know more about this subject should read the previously named book by Dr. Burgmann (see page 89). I must stress the need to avoid food contamination, but what about "homemade" fresh formulas? Be sure especially, that the "use-by" date on human baby foods, for example, has not expired. Work with clean and disinfected utensils; store opened jars in the fridge. Prepared commercial formulas should always be fresh; never use leftovers for the next feed, as they can be a source of contamination. After a time, by trial and error, you will know exactly how much food to prepare for your baby birds. Only portions of formula that are untouched should be stored in the freezer. You may want to send occasional food samples to a laboratory for a bacterial analysis. Find out first how much food they require (usually a minimum of 3.53 ounces [100 g]), how they want it packed, and how they want it shipped (UPS, Federal Express, etc.). Following are names of such laboratories:

A & L Mid West Laboratories, Inc.
13611 "B" Street
Omaha, Nebraska 68144

Hazleton Laboratories America, Inc.
3301 Kinsman Boulevard
Madison, Wisconsin 53704

Woodson-Tenent Laboratories, Inc.
345 Adems Avenue
Memphis, Tennessee 38103

Industrial Laboratories of Canada, Inc.
95 Townline Road
Tillsonburg, Ontario N4G 4H3
Canada

Five-week-old African Gray Parrot.

Foreign Material

It is quite clear that proper digestive functions can be disrupted by bacterial infections as well as by foreign material (bedding, for example), which can block the crop opening. Food that stays too long in the crop will ferment ("sour crop," see page 136). Also, food that is too cold, too dry, too fatty, too high in protein (over 17 percent) or too low in fiber, will disturb the digestive process. Experienced breeders will know that such foods will cause hard lumps in the crop, with unpleasant consequences unless immediate action is taken! Even food that separates itself from the water can give similar problems. We can "dissolve" these lumps by giving the bird a little warm water and giving the crop a massage until the lumps have dispersed.

Badly Formulated Food

Another danger can be caused by feeding with badly formulated food that stays too long in the crop. Small lumps remain in the crop, which practically never empties; this can result in yeast infections (see page 142).

Milk-based Formulas

Milk-based formulas, sooner or later, are not tolerated by some birds, due to an intolerance of lactose. This applies to some psittacines, but I know from years of

Feeding a baby Yellow-fronted Amazon. While facing the chick, offer its food from the left side of its beak. During the feeding process, direct the food toward the right side of the mouth.

experience that not all birds are "anti-milk." I remember well that, in the fifties, I offered milk-soaked bread to tropical finches, canaries, budgerigars, and Australian parakeets, such as rosellas and redrumps. And the parent birds took it to their young by the beakful! I also know (and have personally seen it) that in Mexico and various South American countries, many psittacines are raised on formulas containing milk powder or whole milk. Thus, we can work to a rule of thumb: If the baby birds react well to a milk or milk powder formula—in other words, their droppings are not continually loose and watery—then I see no harm in continuing with it.

Lactose Intolerance

What is the maximum lactose that can be tolerated in a formula? A brief discussion of lactose intolerance is in order here. Lactose or milk-sugar occurs only in milk. It must be broken down into glucose and galactose in the digestive system by the enzyme *lactase*. These monosaccharides can then be absorbed through the intestinal walls into the bloodstream. If too little lactase is available to break down all of the lactose, the remainder will stay in the large intestine and be open to bacterial infection. Such infections include those that cause milk to sour, and that will result in diarrhea. In serious cases, this can include cramps, convulsions, and severe pain. Intestinal irritation can result in the production of extra digestive juices that will inhibit the growth of normal flora bacteria. In chickens, weight loss, increased food and water intake, increased secretion of amino acids, and a decrease in egg production have been determined. There is very little lactase available in the crops of poultry, and there is none at all in the gizzard. Tests with chicks have suggested that lactose should not compose more than 4 percent of the diet. I agree with this figure and would suggest the same for pheasants, quail, and similar species. Higher percentages will cause diarrhea and eventual fatalities.

Vitamins

Vitamins, if used, should be added to the formula after it has been boiled and cooled and is ready to be fed to the chicks. Vitamins are destroyed, or lose a great deal of their strength, if heated.

As you will see in my formula (to the right), I like to work with yogurt or *Lactobacillus acidophilus* to help promote the growth of normal bacterial flora, and to inhibit the growth of yeast, such as *Aspergillus* and *Candida*. Similar products available from reputable pet stores or from health food stores, can be added to the diet after it has been boiled and cooled.

My tip: For the first six days after hatching, I give my baby birds some Ensure Plus, a nutritional product available in health stores, and, as an energy source, one teaspoon of Infalyte, a human electrolyte solution. I mix rice syrup solids with Infalyte/Ensure Plus in a ratio of 75 percent Infalyte/Ensure Plus to 25 percent rice syrup solids (see also page 104).

My tip: The ingredients in the formula (above right) should be blended well together (preferably in an electric blender) until smooth. Then heat in a microwave-safe container to the required temperature of 104 to 110°F (40–43.3°C). I find it better to use it at 104°F (40°C), as crop burns can occur at 105 to

> ## Table 7
> ## Formula for Most
> ## Psittacines
>
> ---
>
> 6 Purina High Protein Monkey Chow biscuits; soaked in water for 20 minutes, then cooked in a microwave oven (or on the stove top).
>
> The cooked biscuits are blended in with the following:
> 3 teaspoons smooth peanut butter
> 3 teaspoons (Gerber's or similar) human oatmeal cereal
> 1 banana
> 3 teaspoons apple sauce
> 3 teaspoons creamed corn human baby food
> 3 teaspoons mixed vegetables human baby food
> 2 teaspoons plain yogurt (or half teaspoon *Lactobacillus acidophilus*)

107°F (40.6–41.7°C), probably due to hot spots at higher temperatures. Although we will be discussing temperatures for baby formulas later (see page 102), I would like to warn about the use of microwaves. They *must* be used cautiously as they tend to heat unevenly and produce hot spots in the formula. If you are only raising a few baby birds, I would advise you to do what I do (I don't take the slightest risk): Mix the food using boiling (and boiled but cooled) water to reach the correct temperature. I use a fast-reading

Table 8
Gower's Aviaries' Formula for Psittacines

Monkey Chow—11.8 ounces (335 g)

Water (distilled)—42.6 ounces (1208 g)

Gerber's Oatmeal Cereal— 3.7 ounces (106 g)

Gerber's Cream Corn— 2.3 ounces (64 g)

Peanut Butter (smooth)— 3.2 ounces (90 g)

Ice cubes—4.6 ounces (130 g)

Soak monkey chow in water 20 to 30 minutes; microwave for 8 minutes.

Add other ingredients, and add ice to cook.

Table 9
Formula for Especially Small Seed-Eating Psittacines, Finches, and Canaries

1.76 ounces (50 g) CéDé or similar commercial rearing food

1.76 ounces (50 g) soybean meal

.42 ounce (12 g) soybean-, corn- or wheat-oil

.14 ounce (4 g) calcium phosphate (food grade)

.04 ounce (1 g) calcium carbonate (food grade)

.07 ounce (2 g) vitamin/mineral supplement

electronic thermometer to monitor the temperature of the formula, and mix it properly.

I am always afraid that a baby will be burned. The first thing that happens is a crop slowdown, then over a period of weeks the crop wall and skin dry out, often eventually falling out, leaving a fistula (a hole connecting the crop to the outside), something that no aviculturist wants to experience!

Case Report

During a study trip to Puerto Rico (Luquillo Forest), I saw, with great admiration, how dedicated people, financed by the U.S. government, were trying to save the Puerto Rico Amazon, *Amazona vittata*, from the brink of extinction. This bird is mainly grass green with a "checked" pattern, and 12 inches (30.5 cm) long. This beautiful Amazon is presently, probably, one of the most endangered Amazon species. Alas, it seems that the bird is still being illegally shot by hunters; in my opinion the Luquillo Forest is much too close to heavily populated areas and the project would be better situated in a more remote spot.

Studies have suggested that this species feeds its young also at night; in the wild many young were found at dawn with full crops. In relation to this, I feed my Amazons until late in the evening and four to eight times per day between 7:00 A.M. and 11:00 P.M., naturally depending on crop emptying. After about three weeks, depending on the species, I feed the birds only three times a day, with the last feed at 10:00 P.M. It takes usually about four hours for the crop to empty completely, as is the case with most cage and aviary birds. If the crop takes six to seven hours to empty completely, something is wrong. The crop is then "washed out" with fluids and massaged, as we discussed on page 137. I always check that the humidity is not too low when I replace the young in the brooder. We will be returning to the rearing of Amazons later (see page 120).

Put formulas into blender and add water to make a smooth texture. If you use a small amount of water or milk, you will get a semi-moist, loose texture that you can use with round-ended (so as not to injure the birds) tweezers. The mixture for baby birds must be warmed (as described above); semimoist food does not need to be so warm; room temperature is adequate.

My tip: As the crop of younger birds is naturally more sensitive to the warm food, I hold the food against my wrist in order to "test" the temperature. With regard to the mixture, I have noticed that baby conures, in particular, do remarkably well if 25 grams (0.9 ounce) of the soybean meal is replaced by 20 grams (0.7 ounce) of potato-protein.

Chapter Six
Feeding Tools and How to Use Them

Introduction

There are various feeding tools used by aviculturists. The decision on what to use is often personal choice. Hand-feeding baby birds is a painstaking job that you should not think of as easy. Faulty tools or faulty use can be dangerous for the birds; therefore, study the various feeding methods used by your colleagues before you feed birds yourself. Years ago I began hand-feeding with various instruments, using sparrows and starlings as "guinea pigs." But you will be able to learn much more quickly if you ask an experienced aviculturist to show you how!

Pipettes

Personally, I like to use a plastic dropper or pipette for tiny birds such as finches, canaries, white-eyes, budgerigars, and mynahs. For finches and similar birds I frequently use glass tools, which are easy to keep clean and will last a long time if used with care. Plastic that is continually in contact with moisture develops tiny cracks that are veritable breeding grounds for all types of bacteria. Glass tools should not be used for larger birds in case of breakage. The formulas we use must be smooth and fluid, to avoid stoppages in the small openings of the tools. Eyedroppers and pipettes (each baby bird should have its own) must be well cleaned and sterilized after each use to prevent bacterial contamination. There are plastic disposable pipettes on the market that may be a little more expensive to use, but they save a lot of time. Pipettes and eyedroppers can be purchased in any drugstore in various sizes and prices. Try to use the best quality; those made of toughened glass or plastic can be boiled to sterilize them.

My tip: Such tools can only be used if the food is evenly emulsified. When you "suck up" the food from the container, be sure you don't get just water, but also the formula itself. It is advisable to run the formula through a blender just before use to get as smooth a mixture as possible. If, after a few days, the young don't seem to be growing satisfactorily, are not putting on enough weight, or are constantly begging for food, you should change to a different pipette with a larger opening, so that you can use a thicker, more substantial formula.

Tube-feeding (Catheter or Tube)

To paraphrase a famous quotation: "To tube-feed or not to tube-feed, that is the question." I would suggest that the potential problems related to tube-feeding could outweigh their benefits, but let us look at their advantages and disadvantages.

There are two types of feeding tube used in aviculture:
- the rubber or plastic catheter tubing that fits on the end of a piston syringe or bulb, and
- the metal feeding tube, that is fastened to the end of a so-called Luer-lock syringe (see Piston Syringes, page 99) and is passed directly into the crop of the baby bird.

Both types of tube make it possible to fill the crop directly from the syringe. All you have to do is fasten the tube to the syringe spout. The food can be syringed into the crop, whether the baby bird wants to eat or not.

I find the benefits of tube-feeding are few, although I will be the first to admit that they save quite some time especially if you have a lot of youngsters to forage. Tube-feeding can be regarded as a "radical" method as,

Tube-feeding a baby cockatiel.

whether right or wrong, the bird cannot refuse to eat. The baby birds don't even get to taste the formula, because the tube always bypasses the taste buds and, as you know, psittacines in particular have a well-developed sense of taste. It is therefore not so surprising that tube-fed babies frequently suffer from stress and all its negative effects.

There are some other difficulties related to tube-feeding. First, it is not out of the question for the tube to separate from the syringe, ending up in the crop, ventriculus, or gizzard. Second, tube-feeding invites the breeder to take an easy way out and to feed several baby birds with the same tool—a sure way of passing on infections. Third, the inside of the tube is very difficult to clean out all food particles, or disinfectants, for that matter! Most fanciers also use the tubes for much too long—long after the inside of the tube can be effectively cleaned. Red rubber tubes harden and crack after a time, forming breeding grounds for pathogens. Also, don't forget that most crop-tubes are opaque, making them difficult to inspect inside. In discussions with aviculturists and avian veterinarians, I find that ignorant use of feeding tubes can lead to lacerations or tears in the mouth lining, the esophagus, or the crop. The only advantage that I can see in tube-feeding is that it can be used to force-feed a baby bird that, for one reason or another, has lost its appetite. In that situation, however, I would recommend that the novice first seek the advice of an avian-veterinarian or experienced aviculturist who is used to hand-feeding baby birds.

I already mentioned the possibility of stress. One of the reasons aviculturists hand-rear baby birds is to get them bonded to humans. I would suggest that tube-feeding as a bonding procedure between the care-giver and the bird is impossible, due to lack of association. When I see how frequently baby birds are tube-raised, as if on a conveyer belt, I ask myself whether dollar-love is greater than bird-love, as I mentioned in the Preface.

Many avian veterinarians are far from happy with tube-feeding, finding that the method is life-threatening to baby birds (infections from improperly disinfected tubes, dislodged tubes resulting in death, or costly surgical procedures, etc.). However, it is possible for an experienced aviculturist or avian veterinarian to help remove a *soft* rubber tube that has lodged in the ventriculus or crop. Such a tube can be removed manually, but you must act quickly!

Case Report

An avian veterinarian friend of mine was consulted by an aviculturist whose ten-week-old Yellow-crowned Amazon, *Amazona ochrocephala*, had swallowed a red rubber feeding tube that had come loose from the syringe. At first, the fancier had assumed the tube would leave the body via "the natural way" and, after the accident, had attempted to feed the bird several times. As he had little success with this, he called the veterinarian some 48 hours later. Shortly after swallowing the tube, the bird began to regurgitate, and, as stated, the feeding (*n.b.* with a tube-feeder!) was far from successful. Can you imagine the stress this poor bird was going through?

The patient was brought to the clinic and, after anesthesia (Isoflurane, Aerrane), an X ray was taken. This showed a lateral view of the tube, which was located in the distal proventriculus as if it were heading for the ventriculus. The veterinarian decided to use clear LRS and 10 percent dextrose for a period of 12 hours, and then proceed with retrieval of the rubber tube via flexible endoscope and grasping claw, again under Isoflurane anesthesia. This procedure took nearly an hour—57 minutes to be exact—luckily with great success, although the tube was difficult to grasp at first.

I think this case report is better than the many words I could write about my feelings with regard to tube-feeding. Admittedly, tube-feeding saves time; but is this an adequate excuse for risking the lives of baby birds? When I think about that baby Amazon, which was lucky to pull through, I realize that a baby bird in our care deserves more than a hasty, painful feeding. Perhaps the aviculturist saved three or four minutes by tube-feeding instead of another method, but the baby Amazon was confronted with physical and emotional stress for 72 hours! In my view, this was a "sick" tradeoff, that deserves a great deal of thought!

Bulb Syringes

This utensil is frequently used to feed larger bird species, such as macaws, African Grays, etc. A bulb syringe has a red rubber bulb fitted to a plastic syringe and "sucks up food" as well as "pushes food out." They are available in several sizes: from 20 cc to 60 cc.

Piston Syringes

These are very popular for feeding small psittacines, such as cock-

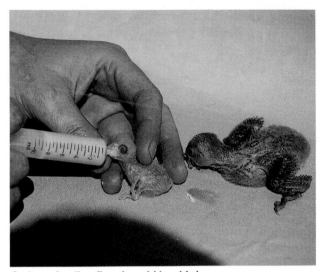
Syringe-feeding five-day-old lovebirds.

atiels, lovebirds, and the smaller conures. They are available in sizes from 0.5 cc to 60 cc, though if you want to use a utensil in excess of 40 cc, I would recommend a bulb syringe. The greatest advantage of a piston syringe is that it is marked,

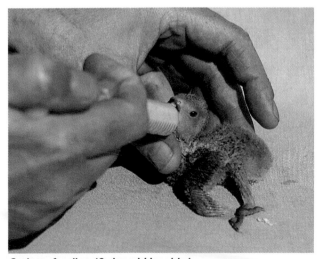
Syringe-feeding 12-day-old lovebirds.

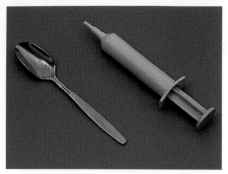

Syringe and bent spoon. To simulate the lower mandible of a parent bird species, the sides of a teaspoon are bent up.

My tip: I like to use the Luer-tip for feeding small birds such as finches, etc., but, I repeat, the formula must, of course, be very smooth. Newly hatched chicks are especially easy (yes, easy!) to feed with this utensil.

Spoon-feeding

From the literature, as well as from other authors, it is well known that I highly recommend the use of a spoon to feed baby birds. Admittedly, it takes longer than other methods, but (and this, I find most important) it is safe for the bird. With spoon-feeding, "the bird itself does the work," and with intensive involvement with the fancier, a special bonding develops. Also, it has become more evident over the years that spoon-feeding leads to easier weaning. As I discussed on page 97, tube-feeding is an impersonal method in which the baby birds don't even get to taste the food so don't know what to expect when they are weaning.

so that you can see exactly how much formula is being used. Moreover, there are two types of tips you can use: the catheter tip and the Luer-tip. The Luer-tip has a smaller outlet and is used primarily in the administration of medicines; the catheter tip has a wider outlet and is thus more suitable for giving a formula, which must, however, be smooth and lump-free.

The sides of a teaspoon (for small bird species I like to use a cocktail spoon) are bent up to form little "gutters" so that the food runs easily from the tip of the spoon without too much spillage. Also, the bent spoon simulates the upper mandible of a "parent" bird. By eating from the spoon, the birds can choose their own "speed" and "rhythm"; they can enjoy the taste of the formula as it touches their taste buds, and can swallow the food slowly without it getting into the windpipe.

Syringe-feeding Black-headed Caiques.

Baby birds used to feeding from a syringe may have difficulties when changing over to a spoon. The "strange" object may scare them. However, the patient aviculturist will soon get them used to it. Patience is indeed a virtue!

My tip: With birds that have never been confronted with a bent spoon, I tap them gently on the beak. This is usually enough to get them begging for food. With the help of a (sterilized) stick, the food can be shoved from the spoon into the mouth. It will definitely please you to see how quickly the birds learn to accept food from a spoon.

A baby Blue-fronted Amazon being spoon-fed.

Gavage Needles

This is a small, stainless steel feeding needle, tipped with a small ball. It is placed directly into the crop. The ball is designed to prevent rupture or penetration of the esophageal wall. After discussions with veterinarians, however, it has become obvious to me that the gavage needle is not an easy instrument to use. In fact, in the hands of a novice it can be a deadly weapon! It is mainly used by experienced breeders for force-feeding sick or weak birds, or for the administration of medicines. In my opinion, a catheter is a better choice for such tasks.

Chapter Seven
Feeding and Weaning Chicks

Introduction

One should not take lightly hand-feeding of baby birds. The food must be at the right temperature (100 to 106°F [37.7–41.1°C]), and not too dry. I am constantly speaking about a smooth formula, without lumps, and I make no excuse for saying it again. Depending on the species and age of the bird, the following moisture percentages apply:

- chicks for the first two to three days: 93 to 95 percent water and 5 to 7 percent solids;
- chicks more than three days of age to weaning age: 75 to 80 percent water and 20 to 25 percent solids. The food can be thickened still further after about three weeks.

As we know, water is the elixir of all life, and therefore of the utmost importance in the rearing of baby birds. They need moisture to avoid dehydration.

The protein levels in the diet should not be too high. We came to the conclusion (see page 88) that an average of 17 percent protein is adequate, as my research over the years has repeatedly shown. If the protein content of the diet is too low (symptoms include slow growth or a globose appearance of the beak), this will lead to, for example, protein deficiency conditions unless the diet is quickly corrected. Fat levels, also, are very important. I have personally found that large birds like macaws, cockatoos, and the larger conures do really well on a fat content of about 12 to 14 percent; smaller bird species will do with a lot less, about 3 to 5 percent fat is adequate.

We have seen that it is more or less impossible to make hard and fast rules about how much food a baby bird should get at each feeding, even though we know the average capacity of various crops (for example, large macaws, 4.39 oz. (130 ml); *Pionus*, 1.18 oz. (35 ml); African Gray, 1.86 oz. (55 ml); Jenday Conure, 0.81 oz. (24 ml); *Pyrrhura* species, 0.51 oz. (15 ml); cockatiels, 0.44 oz. (13 ml); lovebirds, 0.27 oz. (8 ml); budgerigars, 0.24 oz. (7 ml), etc.).

In practice we see that the crop is filled with food. In general, this comes down to the following: for the first four days chicks take about 25 to 28 percent, that is, one quarter to one third of their body weight each day. From 5 to 12 days, as the food becomes increasingly more solid, this drops down to about 15 percent; that means less than one fifth, and will decrease a little further toward weaning. We must be sure that the crop is never overfilled as this can lead to poor crop emptying or even to "droopy crop," which, as Peter Scott, MSc, BVSc, MRCVS, the well-known English avian veterinarian said, "may well need the equivalent of a bra to keep it where it should be."

As we cannot hope to remember everything, we should keep accurate records of each chick's progress (see Record Keeping, page 55). This will obviously include the weight and we should see to it that all birds are weighed at a set time each day. I find the best time is in the morning before the first feed and while the crop is empty. Once the birds have got their pin feathers, it is enough to weigh them every second day. Weighing the birds helps give us an indication of progress. Loss of weight can mean poor digestion or the first sign of illness. We will return to this later (see page 113).

The weaning process, which we will also discuss in this chapter (see pages 113–117), in most cases, poses few difficulties, especially in parrots and parakeets. Weaning means to gradually get the birds used to feeding themselves. In other words, they will no longer be dependent on you to feed them.

Feeding Day-old Baby Birds

Small bird species, in particular, such as canaries, finches, weavers, white-eyes, budgerigars, *Forpus* species, and similar birds are best placed on a high shelf or table at feeding time, so you and the birds are more or less at eye level. In this way you can see better what you are doing, and feed more comfortably. Put the clutch of babies in a sterilized plastic (margarine), or similar square or rectangular container, large enough to hold the clutch, yet small enough to keep them cozy and snuggled together as most species do naturally in the nest. Put paper towels, tissues, or wood shavings, free of dust, in the bottom of the container to avoid splayed legs. A few wads of tissue

Young parakeets, 2 to 4 days old.

Young parakeets, 12 days old.

can also be strategically placed in the nest to give the chicks somewhere to rest their chins after feeding (see Important Note on next page). One or more heat sources, such as an office lamp with a swinging arm and a 100 watt bulb will keep the chicks in the container warm, as well as the one that is being fed. Chilled babies will usually refuse to eat. Study the Important Note on the next page.

My tip: I assist one- to three-day-old chicks to stay upright by holding the head between my fingers. Young chicks of larger species rarely need to be helped in this manner. With this "assistance," the bird's neck is stretched up making it open its beak. With most species of hook-bills, the upper mandible is plainly somewhat larger than the lower mandible, with its edge "folded round" the lower mandible. If a chick refuses to open its beak, I let a little "liquid" food run along the left side

of the upper mandible so that it trickles into the lower mandible. The bird will then acquire a taste for the formula and will, the next time, usually open its beak for a feed. With this "trickle method," hold the bird's head up with thumb and forefinger so that the head and neck are more or less in alignment. I feed hatchlings up to the third day, at least every two hours, from 6:00 A.M. to midnight. When feeding very young birds, I wear disposable surgical gloves in order to avoid contamination as much as possible.

Let's return to our discussion about feeding day-old baby birds. The very first feeding for a newly hatched chick—after it has completely dried out, which may take several hours—consists of just a few drops of boiled (and cooled to the required temperature) water, together with an electrolyte solution, to give the chick a boost. Personally, I use Infalyte together with Ensure Plus, which is vanilla flavored, in a 50:50 solution. After the second day all chicks get a daily dose of the mixture named on page 93 until they are a week old (given, for example, one hour before the second feeding of the morning). For this information, I am thankful to the aviculturists Voren and Jordan who, in their book *Parrots, Hand Feeding and Nursery Management*, state: "Very small chicks may take as little as .1 or .2 cc where larger chicks may take up to one full milliliter on the first feeding. The vast majority of parrots that are raised will usually fall into the .25

to .5 milliliter category. With each feeding there is a need to stretch or dilate the crop just a little. When feeding solely liquid, care must be taken not to aspirate the chicks. Thinned formula is less likely to be aspirated but the risk is present when using either diet."

Feeding Older Chicks

As we have said, there are usually no difficulties with regard to formula feeding. Occasionally, a chick will refuse to open its beak. If that happens, you might try the following techniques:

- gently press or tap the feeding tool on the top or sides of the beak;
- gently tap near the notched part of the upper mandible (many psittacines have a notched upper mandible);
- stroke with the index finger over the head, neck, or back (make sure your hands are warm and that the warmth "flows" through your rubber gloves);
- press a warm, hand-feeding spoon against the corner of the

Important Note

By lightly tapping the upper beak with the feeding spoon, or by carefully stretching the neck up (you will then have a clear view of the birds crop), you will encourage the bird to open its beak. At the same time, it will move its head (so-called head bobbing).

Now is the time to place the tip (a small tip is best) of the feeding tool into the bird's beak.

The best position for the feeding tool is the left of the baby's beak angled down to the right, hence next to your left hand. This position—providing you don't "jam" the syringe in—makes it possible to guide the formula down into the chick's crop, away from the opening to its lungs. As soon as the food enters the mouth, the head bobbing increases, making it easier to swallow. Once the food is swallowed, the bird will be able to take a good breath, before the next portion of food is given. When the bird stops bobbing its head, it is usually a sign that the bird has eaten enough. Check the crop; when well filled it should be like a soft ball. It should *never* be a taut bulge.

If the crop is not full enough, give the chick a little time to work the food before offering more. Once the chick has had enough to eat, it should be cleaned up with a soft tissue or cotton ball and warm water, so that no food residue is left to harden on the beak or body. Formulas quickly get hard, and dirty chicks placed back in the nest with their siblings can cause all sorts of problems, bearing in mind that spoiled formula is a breeding ground for bacteria.

Two-week-old Zebra Finches.

mouth or against various parts of the upper mandible (take note that not every bird, even of the same

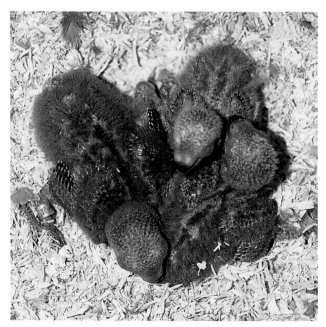
Young lovebirds.

species, reacts to the same impulse on a particular spot; thus, if a bird reacts positively to a touch on the left side of the upper mandible, it does not mean that a related bird will react positively at the same spot).

As the chicks get older, their demand for food will increase and they will open their beaks as soon as they notice your approach. Always be sure the formula is given at the correct temperature (see page 102). Experience has shown that not all youngsters are happy with food brought to a certain temperature. Sometimes it can be a bit frustrating when not all chicks in the same clutch will accept food at the same temperature, especially when you are spoon-feeding. You will have to experiment, by trial and error, until all of the young are feeding happily. Of course, this makes hand-feeding all the more interesting and challenging—and don't forget to keep notes!

As we have frequently seen, the consistency of the formula should pose few problems. Very young birds require a great deal of moisture (see page 93) so, for the first few days, the formula is thinner than that given to older birds. By using a bent spoon to feed, we can, of course, give a thicker formula than we could by tube-feeding. When feeding, it is advisable to observe the esophageal canal, which is situated on the right side of the neck, where it enters the crop. Once the crop is more or less full, the food can easily be seen in the esophageal canal. If this is running quickly, the chick will be able to take more food; if it runs slowly, the crop will be full. At this point, it is advisable to slow down, and to stop feeding once the food is hardly moving in the esophageal canal.

We must take every precaution not to overfill the crop. If this should happen, we should suck out a little food from the crop with the aid of a tube (see page 136). A sudden increase in the quantity of formula is not recommended. Increase amounts gradually, and see that the crop can be emptied comfortably in two to four hours. If the crop suddenly takes longer to empty, you may be giving too much food, or the formula may be too dry. As a rule of thumb, we can assume that most small bird species, such as finches and canaries in the second week, and budgerigars (parakeets), cockatiels, *Neophema* species, lovebirds, etc. in the third week, have reached the point where the crop cannot take a further increase in food. Larger bird species reach maximum crop capacity in about 3½ weeks, while in large macaws and similar-sized bird species it may take 8 to 12 weeks.

Body Development

Note that it is not only the crop that is developing—the whole body of the bird is, in a rush to grow to adulthood. After the first week we will see the appearance of the pin feathers in many bird species, and

Hungry Plum-headed Finches.

the somewhat unattractive chick transforms itself quickly into a bird. This body development requires adequate food, and it is understandable that the food intake gradually increases at each feeding. This means that the crop will take a little longer to empty and the number of

A week-old Parrotlet.

African Gray Parrot, raised by the author.

feeds can be decreased. At a certain time the chick will have food in its crop some hours after a feed. Food that is in the crop for 10 to 12 hours has a tendency to sour, resulting in so-called "sour-crop"

Severe Macaw (Ara severa) babies.

(see page 136). In such cases we must reduce the amount of food given immediately. Personally, I have had much success when I give smaller portions of formula but increase the feedings by two or three. Don't forget to note all changes, and any related consequences, in your records.

Methods of Feeding Chicks

We have already discussed the advantages and disadvantages of hand-feeding tools (see Chapter 6). I made no secret of the fact that I consider the feeding spoon to be the best method, but I realize that the breeder of many bird species must resort to tube-feeding or something similar.

Spoon-feeding is slow, as we know, but it is safer and more personal. Take the spoon in one hand. With the thumb and forefinger of the other hand, gently grasp the head, especially of small bird species, and line it up with the neck. Grip the head just behind the eyes, which appear as dark circles in newly hatched young. It should not take long before the chicks gape for food automatically when they hear you, so that you can carefully roll the food into the open beak one drop at a time. At a later time, depending on the bird species, the birds will eat the food from the spoon themselves. Some birds occasionally do not eat enough at feeding time, in which case the number of feeds should be increased.

Feeding spoons should be handled with care and held as vertically as possible so that they are more or less in line with the head and neck of the baby bird. Under no circumstances must the baby birds get food into the lungs, so syringes must be used with great caution. The feeding tube should enter the chick's beak on the left (while the bird is "facing" you) and pass over the tongue to the right rear of the mouth, the esophagus. This is the entrance to the crop that is opened and closed with a pumping action to draw in the food. After the first day, or as soon as the baby birds open their beaks automatically to be fed, it is possible to inject food with a syringe, or a similar instrument, directly into the crop. If the food runs back into the mouth, you are feeding too quickly and you should stop immediately. Wait until the bird has swallowed the food before starting to feed again with the feeding tool.

A healthy Goffin's Cockatoo (Cacatua goffini).

Feeding Difficulties

Experience has shown that birds that are not immediately removed from the parents' nest, sometimes have difficulties after hatching. Birds that are removed to the nursery immediately after hatching seldom have problems, but baby birds from a few days to a week old that have been fed by their parents will refuse to be hand-fed. By gently tapping the beak with the feeding spoon (see page 105), you can usually get them to open their mouths. Young psittacines have a habit of lying on their backs and making defensive movements with their feet. Sometimes they roll over after feeding, with the danger that the food is lost from the crop into the mouth. There is also a great danger that the food will enter the airpipe and cause aspiration and even death! Such birds must be carefully monitored for a day after the feeding.

Force-feeding: Tools and Techniques

Baby birds that refuse to eat normally must receive special attention.

Cut-throat Finches (Amadina fasciata) *being hand-fed.*

Such birds can often only be saved by force-feeding. The best tools for this are the tube or the catheter. Use only soft rubber tubing with a diameter a little less than that of the esophagus. New tubing is often soft and difficult to control, so work cautiously. The length of the tube is also important; one that is too long

Four-week-old Senegal Parrots (Poicephalus senegalus).

will drive you crazy! The tip of the tube must always be pushed into the opening of the esophagus, taking care not to cause discomfort to the bird. The length of the chosen tube can be determined as follows: Measure from the beak and along the neck to the middle of the crop (draw an imaginary line from the middle of the crop to the tube). For safety's sake, I add two inches (5.1 cm) to the measurement. The tip that passes into the esophagus must never be "sharp." For this reason, I don't favor the gavage needle (see page 101), especially in the hands of inexperienced beginners. A rubber tip can be made smooth by holding a lighted match to it, after which it must be thoroughly cleaned and disinfected.

The bird is held in the same way as when we are using other feeding tools. If it is a bird that refuses to feed or won't open its beak, you may need the help of a second person. One person holds the bird in one hand in the typical upright position, but with thumb and forefinger on either side of the bird's jaw, just at the corners of the beak. With the application of a little pressure, the chick should open its beak. The other hand is used to steady the bird and to stop it from flipping over onto its back. Under no circumstances should pressure be applied to the beak itself during the feeding session, as this may result in permanent compression of the lower mandible, or a lateral deviation of the upper mandible. The second person can now place the tube in the correct position; I like to lubricate the tube with K-Y Jelly (commercially available), or with warm distilled water. You hold the syringe in the right hand, provided you are right-handed, otherwise in the left hand, and feed the chick from the left. It is advisable to use your left index finger as an anchor while feeding the chick, in order to have some control over the tube—it is not unknown for sudden movements to result in puncture wounds! In this respect it is worth mentioning that some psittacines are vigorous feeders, especially macaws and large conures, which often receive puncture crop wounds from pumping too forcefully on the syringe. However, it is safe to feed the baby bird when it is pumping because the trachea is closed at that time, as we already have mentioned.

The catheter is also often used for force-feeding. It is passed directly into the esophagus opening. Again, it is recommended that two people should be involved with catheter feeding.

Growth Rates

It goes without speaking that our aim is to raise healthy birds, with a minimum weight loss; however, we use a certain formula, *not* to increase the chick's growth rate but, with correct feeding, to let the bird develop properly and naturally. To monitor the growth rate of our birds, we should weigh them each

Two hand-raised Rose-breasted Cockatoos (Cacatua roseicappilus).

morning before the first feeding, when the crop is empty.

As the chick gets older (as we have said several times), the feeding method changes and there will be longer periods between feeding sessions. Once this period starts, more food is given at each session, but feeding sessions are reduced by two or three times.

Baby birds that are developing well can be recognized by the following:

• a chubby body; toes and wings, especially the "elbows," have a well-developed appearance; they should not, under any circumstances be thin;

• a keel bone that should not protrude; the breast is well rounded;

• a skin that should be well hydrated, pinkish, flesh-colored, soft to the touch, and somewhat translucent (especially easy to see at the crop and underbody).

111

Young lovebirds, enjoying a large flight.

Baby birds, even from the same clutch, often show marked variations in weight; therefore, each bird is given its own record page or card, where the daily and weekly development is noted. Weigh your bird and transfer the results to a graph (see samples, pages 114 and 115). The easiest way is to show the age of the chick, in days, on the horizontal axis and the body weight, in grams, on the vertical axis.

A healthy chick generally gains weight every day, although the amount of weight gain is naturally not equal every day. As long as the weight increase is adequate, however, and the baby is healthy (according to the points given above), there is no need to worry. A sick baby will seldom gain weight, and is more likely to lose some,

often a few days before other symptoms become apparent, so weight loss is a good sign that a bird is becoming ill. In the case of weight loss with no apparent cause, it is best to consult an avian veterinarian.

If you decide to keep weight charts—and I certainly advise you to—purchase a good set of easy-to-read, digital gram scales. Many models have a perch for weighing older birds and a basket for weighing chicks. If you can afford it, it will pay to buy scales that weigh in 1 gram increments; these are much more accurate than those that weigh in increments of 2 grams or more. It should not have to be said that scales, including the perch and the basket, must be kept as clean and sterile as all other equipment you use in your nursery.

Parakeets come in many different colors and color combinations.

Weaning

The time will come when the baby birds no longer need to be fed with feeding tools. It is difficult to put a set time on when various species of birds begin to take solid food; however, recognizing the right time to start weaning is a challenge that requires much patience and careful observation by the aviculturist. Finches and canaries, for example, begin to look for seeds and other more or less solid food as soon as they are feathered; therefore, I offer such birds sprouted millet or millet spray, and rearing food (CéDé, for instance). Lories and lorikeets pose few difficulties, as they continue to live on a formula similar to that on which they are reared. A heavy, shallow, earthenware bowl (so it cannot be tipped over when the birds perch on the rim) is placed low down in the brooder or cage, so that the birds can get accustomed to it. After two days, the bowl is filled with formula. Many breeders leave the feeding spoon or other tool in the bowl to make the food even more familiar to the birds, so that they will begin to eat independently and avoid stress.

Weight Loss

During the feeding process we see rapid changes in the body, such as feather growth, and especially the

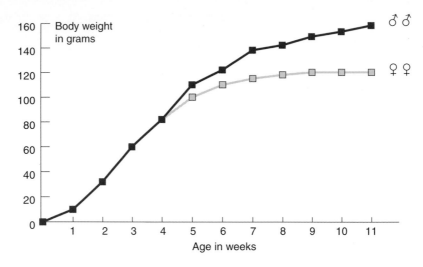

Typical growth curve for a Japanese Quail (Coturnix japonica) *(after Holsheimer).*

shrinking of the crop to that of adult size of the species in question. In spite of this, we must continually check that the birds are eating adequately. We can only consider that the weaning process is complete when the bird is able to eat enough "solid" food to maintain its own body weight for three consecutive days. We must not forget, however, that birds in the weaning process may lose up to 10 percent body

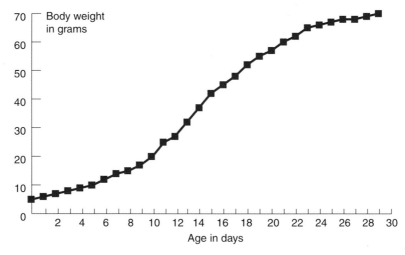

Typical growth curve for a hand-fed Red-rumped Parakeet (Psephotus haematonotus) *(after Holsheimer).*

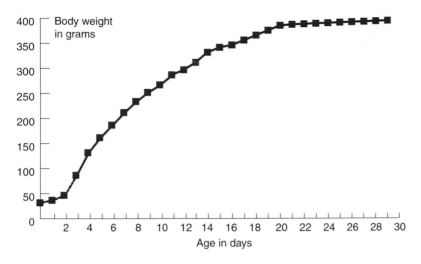

Typical growth curve for a hand-fed Wood Pigeon (Columba palumbus) *(after Holsheimer).*

weight during the "pre-flight weight loss." This is easy to understand: In the wild, baby birds are extremely well fed by their parents, and the chicks lose little energy, as they are simply sitting in the nest and they grow quickly. Just before fledging time, they often weigh more than either parent, but the pre-flight weight loss, which also occurs in hand-reared birds, is nothing more than a preparation for flight.

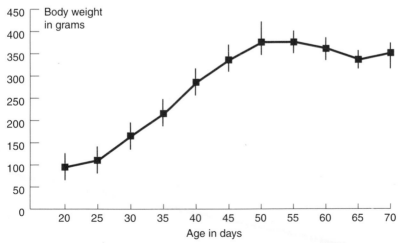

Typical growth curve for three hand-fed Orange-winged Amazons (Amazona amazonica). *The slight loss of weight (the curve goes downward) occurred at weaning time (fifty-fifth day), when the birds started to eat on their own (Zoonooz, August 1978).*

Apart from losing weight, the bird must be alert, lively, and in full color. Stools must not be dark in color; they must be moist and plentiful. If a baby bird loses more than 10 percent of its body weight, if the stools are dark green and dry, or sparse, if the bird is lethargic and continually begging for food, if it has a swollen crop that stays full for too long, or does not completely empty, it is high time to take it to an avian veterinarian.

The weaning process for most non-nectar- or fruit-eating psittacines is between four and eight weeks of age (exceptions are, for example, the large macaws). In this period, the birds start to peck at small, dark objects that are on a lighter background, and try to eat them. As soon as you see them doing this, it is time to give them some easily digestible bits of food to peck up. The food must be placed within their reach. For this reason it is best to use light-colored kitchen towels in the brooder as bedding.

Food to Start With

At this stage I like to give my birds soft egg food (CéDé, for example), soaked in milk or water (and then squeezed out), whole-wheat bread, and pellets softened with apple juice. All these foodstuffs will stimulate self-feeding behavior. Once the birds have been busy with this food for a few days (but with hand-feeding continuing), you can offer them soaked and sprouted seeds, millet spray, pieces of cheese, willow twigs, and pieces of apple, in addition to the food mentioned above. Since the food is given in the paper towel bedding, these must be renewed frequently, because the birds step on it and soil it, and we don't want them to eat soiled food. Keep the birds' beaks and toes as clean as possible.

Drinking Water

Once the birds are feeding themselves, they must have constant access to fresh drinking water (brought to room temperature). Always put the water in a heavy drinking bowl that the birds cannot tip over. You can dissolve some avian vitamin/mineral supplement in the water, which should be changed several times a day; however, avoid too much vitamin D_3 for young macaws and cockatiels (D_3 toxicosis). You can hang a water bottle in the cage or brooder next to the water dish. Since birds are naturally inquisitive, it will not be long before they learn to drink from it. Once the birds are able to obtain sufficient water from the bottle, you can dispense with the water bowl. The water bottle must be regularly cleaned and sterilized to prevent buildup of pathogenic organisms. Because old aquarium tanks are easy to clean, and are good for monitoring birds, I also like to use these for weaning. Use only tissue as substrate, not corncobs, walnut shells, or cedar shavings, which the birds may eat, with gizzard compaction resulting.

Other Signs of Weaning Time

There are, of course, other signs that indicate the approach of weaning time. One of the most obvious is when the birds struggle during tube-feeding, or enthusiastically take the food from the feeding spoon themselves, rather than let you "roll it into their mouths." The struggle will gradually become more serious and may include rolling on the back and kicking with the feet. In short, the birds make a fuss and refuse to let you feed them; they will let you hand-feed them only if they are really hungry. Once the birds become difficult to hand-feed, you can stop and allow them to eat "off the floor." Now add dry pellets, easy-to-de-hull seeds (millets, hemp, canary seed, etc.) and de-hulled sunflower seeds (but not too many of these!), oats and groats, wheat, greens and fruits, thin willow branches (about 3 inches [7.6 cm] in length), egg food (such as CéDé), millet spray, and other tidbits, depending on the bird species. Check your bird books for what particular species need in their menus.

When to Dispense with Hand-feeding

You should inspect the birds' crops to ensure they are eating enough; if more than one third full, you can dispense with hand-feeding. In any case, the amounts given by hand-feeding should be slowly reduced. Many breeders eliminate first the lunchtime formula, then breakfast, and finally the evening feeding. Roudybush believes that weaning is a developmental and not a learned process. I agree, but would also say that delayed weaning is often caused by poor growth and/or malnutrition. You should, therefore, not be alarmed if weaning takes a little longer than stated in textbooks. Dr. Burgmann, DVM, correctly states: "Nonetheless, a problem that I see frequently in my practice are birds that are still being hand-fed far past the normal age of weaning. This occurs because owners do not catch on to the typical weaning signals and continue to force-feed the baby until the baby loses the desire to fend for itself and becomes dependent on the hand-feeding. Once this occurs, weaning becomes far more difficult. One way to start to break this cycle is to offer warm food in a dish, and hold the dish up in front of the bird until it begins to show the feeding response. As soon as it shows the feeding response, lower the dish to the floor and leave the bird to eat on its own. It is important to leave it for a little while, or your presence will distract the bird and stimulate it to continue to beg. Continue to do this during the day, but if by evening the bird is still begging and has an empty crop, do feed it, although you should be gradually decreasing the amount of feeding per meal."[1]

---

[1]Petra Burgmann, D.V.M., *Feeding Your Pet Bird* (Hauppauge: Barron's Educational Series, 1993).

Chapter Eight
Hand-feeding Step-by-Step (Practical Notes)

Introduction

It is perhaps useful and interesting to present a few notes taken from a selection of the many bird species I have raised in my nursery. There are no fast rules and guarantees for absolute success. I have made no secret of the fact that "if *your* care and management produces excellent results, then you must go your own way—you don't need to listen to the ideas of others (hence, also not mine); let your success continue!"

The following notes are thus in no way designed to make the reader into a specialist. In the not too distant past, hand-rearing was primarily used to save young birds that would otherwise be doomed. Rare species, especially species in which adults are known to be bad parents under captive conditions were the next to be hand-raised. Today, unfortunately, we see countless numbers of nestlings hand-reared for the pet trade. What we once did

for love, in short to save the bird, has resulted all too frequently in hand-feeding and -rearing baby birds for purely commercial purposes—and aviculture gets the blame for it!

Many species of psittacines, such as cockatiels, various conure species, and some lovebirds, are mass-produced for the pet trade. These species have been more or less domesticated for many years and are not as sensitive as many other cage and aviary birds. Also, such birds are not exposed to the danger of having the breeder degrade the hens to "egg-laying machines," and take each egg away for artificial incubation. Unfortunately, this does happen with many very sensitive and nervous species, especially Amazons, cockatoos, and macaws.

I think it is absolutely necessary to allow every pair of birds, *at least every second year*, to rear their own clutch of youngsters. Otherwise, there is a very real danger of hand-reared birds totally losing their parental instincts, a fact that many in the pet trade fail to realize. Another misconception is that birds should be sold before they are fully weaned, with the excuse that they will become "imprinted" on people. Such birds, once adult, are usually quite unsuitable for breeding. Fortunately, one can avoid this by placing young of the same species together in the same brooder or cage, and thus not raise them individually. Keep siblings together, even when hand-feeding. Many bird species, especially cockatoos (with the exception of Moluccan Cockatoo), have no fear of humans after the weaning period, but are not particularly "familiar." Most Moluccan Cockatoos that I have studied in the wild, and the few that I have hand-reared, were exceptionally friendly, quickly became "attached," and continued to show "attention and friendship." With regard to the hand-fed babies, this affection was demonstrated particularly during and after feeding. Various conures show a similar type of behavior. I solved the problem of "human-attached" birds by separating them from the others in the nursery and placing them where they could see and hear adults of their own species (often their own parents).

Temperament Differences

In general, hand-reared birds are somewhat calmer than those that are

Sixty-day-old Moluccan Cockatoo (Cacatua moluccensis) *hand-fed and raised by the author.*

reared naturally, and are less likely to suffer stress. It is important that such hand-reared and weaned birds, especially endangered species, are used for breeding when the time is ripe, so that we will continue to keep the species for aviculture and our descendants. Unfortunately, there is one negative aspect—birds that have little or no fear of the aviculturist, and are normally on the best of terms with him or her, can become extremely aggressive in the breeding season, especially when they have eggs or young. Disturb your birds as little as possible during this period, as their aggression can be redirected at their own young, resulting in mutilation and fatalities. This is particularly apparent in cockatoos. In such cases you must, of course, save the youngsters and rear them yourself. If

This Leadbeater's Cockatoo (Cacatua leadbeateri) *was bred and raised by the author.*

the birds only have eggs, I replace these with artificial or infertile ones that I remove when the incubation period has lapsed. This prevents the hen from laying another clutch, and becoming a laying machine, with all its unfortunate consequences (think, for example, about egg binding and loss of condition). Also, you have more chance of fertile eggs if you let nature take its own course. Female

birds can only produce a certain number of eggs in their lives. If there are no more eggs left in the ovary, then it cannot produce any more, even when the bird is in its prime of life.

Hand-feeding and weaning baby birds is indeed a task requiring total commitment, and a love and understanding of the birds.

Hand-feeding Amazon Parrots

Amazon parrot hatchlings, of various species, are given the formula described on page 93 after they have produced their first droppings. Thereafter, they are given the formula found on page 93. The birth weight of Amazon parrots varies between 10 grams (0.35 oz.) and 28 to 31 grams (.99–1.09 oz.). The brooder should be maintained at 97°F (36.1°C) for the first four days; over the next three weeks the temperature is gradually reduced (in four to five days) to 90°F (32.2°C). I prefer to place clutches from the same nest together in a brooder (most Amazons lay three or more eggs per clutch). Once the young get their pin feathers, the temperature is further reduced to 86°F (30°C). Most Amazon parrots can be leg-banded at three weeks of age. Use only stainless steel bands, as other bands quickly deteriorate and can cause wounds.

During the first week after hatching, all the chicks are fed with a good liquid formula from a pipette or syringe, every 2½ hours starting at 7:00 A.M. and ending at 10:30 P.M. Hard deposits sometimes form in the crops of Amazon parrots (and in many other bird species), if they are fed with a too dry diet. This is not too much of a problem if we take action within the hour. Keep the bird hydrated. The well-known English Amazon experts Pat and John Stoodley advise the use of Ringer's solution, or just warm water, "given for a few hours, and followed later by an energizing liquid such as rice water." Rice water is invaluable in the nursery according to these aviculturists, and I thoroughly agree with them. To make rice water, put a heaped teaspoon of round grain rice in a pint (0.47 L) of water and boil it until the rice is well broken down; then strain out the residue. Give this to the bird at the feeding times stated above for two days; other food is not necessary. On the third day, offer the formula again, this time made up with rice water. The following day you can return to the normal formula. Sometimes lumps in the crop are a symptom of *candidiasis* (see page 134), in which case an avian veterinarian should be consulted.

As soon as the chicks get their pin feathers, you can place slices of sweet apple and other fruit, some greens, and millet spray at the eye level of the youngsters in the brooder to encourage self-feeding. Once they start eating this, you can give them a bowl of fruit slices.

Hand-fed baby Blue and Gold Macaw **(Ara ararauna),** *10 weeks old.*

Make sure the bowl is heavy, with a solid rim, so that it doesn't move or tip when the birds sit on it. You can also give them a bowl of sprouted

Moluccan cockatoos **(Cacatua moluccensis);** *the oldest chick is 21 days, the youngest a week.*

Growing up rapidly.

Hand-feeding Blue and Gold Macaws

My first youngsters were reared in a still-air incubator as follows: The temperature in the incubator was maintained at 90°F (32.2°C) with the relative humidity set at 65 percent. At hatching time, this was increased to 70 percent. The eggs were turned five times per day, and ventilated for seven minutes. After the first evacuation of the bowel (which can take 12 to 24 hours), they were given 0.5 ml formula. This was gradually increased over a month to 0.7 to 1.1 ounce (20–30 g) per feed. The first formula, given for two days, was the one on page 93. Feeding times were: 6:00 A.M., 8:30 A.M., 11:00 A.M., 1:30 P.M., 4:00 P.M., 6:30 P.M., 9:00 P.M., and 11:30 P.M. The formula for the third and fourth days was that given on page 93, with the same feeding times. On the fifth to seventh days, the formula was bolstered with 1.75 ounces (50 g) of milled sunflower kernels and the feeding times were 6:00 A.M., 9:00 A.M., noon, 3:00 P.M., 6:00 P.M., and 9:00 P.M.

At one to three weeks the same formula was given, but with the addition of 8.8 ounces (250 g) of oatmeal, and moistened with apple pulp and finely grated carrot in a 50:50 mixture. In the second week I also mixed in a little chopped greenfood. Feeding times were 6:00 A.M., 9:00 A.M., noon, 3:00 P.M., 6:00 P.M., and 9:00 P.M.

seeds, germinated pulses, chopped vegetables and greens, sweet corn, 3-inch-long (7.6 cm) willow twigs, green peas, and a few hulled sunflower seeds. The millet spray should be available at eye level at all times in the brooder so that the birds can peck at it and learn how to de-hull seeds, as they should also soon do with the sunflower seeds. Once the young birds are eating adequately, two hand-feedings (12:00 P.M. and 4:00 P.M.) will suffice.

Many bird breeders let the parents rear the young to pin feather stage, then start hand-feeding them. Not all chicks will readily accept food from a spoon or syringe, so you will require a great deal of patience! If the bird remains unwilling, you may have to resort to force-feeding. Young birds may, understandably, lose weight at this time, but as soon as they are ready to accept hand-feeding, they will put the weight back on.

From the third to the sixth week I kept the same formula but increased the milled sunflower kernels to 3.5 ounces (100 g). Feeding times were 7:00 A.M., 10:00 A.M., 1:30 P.M., 5:30 P.M., 8:30 P.M. and 11:30 P.M. After the fourth week feeding times were reduced to four per day, at 8:00 A.M., noon, 4:00 P.M., and 10:30 P.M.

The menu after the seventh week was still similar, but with .35 ounce (10 g) of finely ground oyster grit added. Once a day I replaced one of the baby "ingredients" with cooked and finely shredded chicken meat. The consistency of the food was similar to that of yogurt. The feeding times were 8:00 A.M., 4:00 P.M., and 8:30 P.M. I kept to the principle that the young birds' crops should be full at night, and empty in the morning before the first feed. My young macaws ate about 3.5 ounces (100 g) of food each a day at seven to eight weeks of age. The birds were monitored closely and, if the crop was empty too soon at any time, a little extra feed was given. As you will have noticed, the noon meal was stopped at the seventh week.

With effect, from the tenth week, I began the weaning process seriously. A week earlier, I had started to give the young various tidbits to peck at, but toward the end of the tenth week, the birds were going to sleep with crops full of self-eaten food. I gave them half-ripe corn, germinated seeds, soft fruit, and a continuous supply of sorghum millet. I kept to the following routine:

Four-week-old Yellow-crowned Amazon, subspecies **Amazona ochrocephala tresmariae.**

- in the morning the birds were offered half-ripe corn, germinated seeds, and pellets softened with apple juice;
- in the afternoon they were offered finely sliced apple, pieces of banana, and germinated seeds;
- in the evening they were offered the familiar, but now loose hand-feeding formula, enriched with some vitamin/mineral supplement and hard seeds (I used a good brand of parrot mixture).

The formula given per spoon had a temperature of 99°F (37.2°C). With one chick, I used a syringe for the first few days. Opening the beak posed no difficulties; a light tap on the upper beak with a spoon made them open their beaks automatically. After each feeding I cleaned the beak, crop, and breast thoroughly to remove any spillages.

Weight Record

The following is an interesting example of a weight record. A young Blue and Gold Macaw was brought to me because it refused to eat. On the day it was brought to me it was 11 days old and weighed only 1.6 ounce (45 g). I decided to feed it with a syringe. On the thirty-third day I changed to spoon feeding.

The bird did very well and grew into a magnificent, healthy specimen. As soon as he was eating independently, his favorite food next to seed and pellets was cracked walnuts, long, pencil-thin carrot strips, large spinach leaves, and approximately 6-inch-long (15 cm) celery sticks. As the bird always ate this food so enthusiastically, I introduced it to the menu given to the other baby macaws. As soon as the bird was completely independent, he was given a bowl of mixed seeds with his pelleted food (he found it very entertaining to crack seeds and to play with them). I also gave him pieces of apple, orange, grapes, bananas, and papaya.

Hand-feeding Lories and Lorikeets

The following are just a handful of general notes, as most lories and lorikeets are hand-raised on more or less the same food they eat as adults.

I am all for letting the parent birds rear the young for the first two or three weeks—large species two weeks, small species (Goldies and similar species) three weeks. Before moving the chicks to the brooder, they are banded. I keep the brooder temperature at 85°F (29.4°C), and the relative humidity at 47 percent. Because of their thin droppings, I use cut-to-size grocery bags, dull side up, as underlay on the brooder floor, and heavy kitchen towels as bedding. After each feeding the two "carpet" layers are renewed. The brooder is cleaned with bleach and water, and disinfected with Novassan every day. The birds are replaced when the brooder is dry. I use a hair dryer to speed things up.

Table 10 Weight Record	
Age (days)	Weight in ounces (grams)
13	1.9 (55)
15	2.3 (65)
17	3.2 (90)
19	3.4 (96)
21	3.6 (103)
23	4.0 (114)
25	4.5 (129)
27	4.8 (138)
29	5.9 (169)
31	7.0 (200)
33	8.2 (235)
35	9.8 (280)
37	10.5 (300)
39	12.0 (340)
41	13.1 (375)
43	14.2 (405)
45	15.2 (435)
47	17.7 (505)

As spoon-feeding is so messy (the food is so thin), I use a syringe or a 4-ounce (120 cc) paper cup. One of the advantages of using these inexpensive feeding utensils is that the thickness of the rim is suitable for all lory and lorikeet species. For hand-feeding I use, after the first day (on the first day after the first bowel movement I use the formula described on page 93), the commercial lory food that is also given to the adult birds. All I add to this is a little finely ground cuttlefish bone. The mixture must be adequately fluid (consistency of natural yogurt) and it is warmed to 100°F (37.8°C) and stirred so that there are no hot spots in it that could cause crop burn. The paper cup is half-filled with formula and offered to the bird. Once it starts to eat, I tilt the cup slightly up so that a stream of food flows into the bird's mouth. To avoid cross-contamination, each baby bird has its own cup. After use I throw the cups away. I begin the feedings at 7:00 A.M. and continue at 10:00 A.M., 3:00 P.M., 7:00 P.M., and 11:00 P.M.

At about seven weeks to three months of age I give the birds nectar, in a separate paper cup (again, each bird has its own cup), at the 3:00 P.M. feed, in addition to the formula. They get the nectar from the cup for two days, then I present it in an open bowl with a wide rim, again after the fourth feeding, and one hour before the last feeding. They are also given finely chopped vegetables and cubes of fruit as a supplement in a separate bowl.

The "tresmariae" subspecies in the wild is restricted to Trés Maria Islands, western Mexico.

From this point, the formula can also be given in a bowl. Personally, I often (depending on how the birds react) give them vegetables and fruit with the nectar in the same bowl. At approximately three months of age, the birds are offered a dry commercial lory diet, but they still get the nectar, fruit, and vegetables, and the "liquid" formula respectively.

Hand-feeding *Pionus* Species

As many *Pionus* species are quite rare in the wild and still endangered (I am thinking here especially about the White-headed or Massena Pionus, *Pionus tumultous seniloides*), I regularly hand-reared the young, in spite of the fact that I find most of the adults make excellent parents that rear their young well. All species that I have reared were often taken from their parents after 12 to 15 days. All

Two Lesser Sulphur-crested Cockatoos (Cacatua s. sulphura), *bred and raised by the author; 40 and 48 days respectively.*

species are fed with the same formula (see page 93), and the feeding times are the same. The temperature of the formula is maintained at 103°F (39.4°C) and the protein content brought up to about 17 percent by the addition of three teaspoons

The same youngsters, now 51 and 59 days old, respectively.

of finely ground sunflower kernels (about 14.5 percent protein).

At the very first feeding, the birds were given the formula described on page 93. I gave each baby bird about 10 cc after the first bowel evacuation. The chicks were fed at 7:00 A.M., 11:00 A.M., 3:00 P.M., 7:00 P.M., and 11:00 P.M. At 14 to 15 days old they received four feeds: 7:00 A.M., noon, 3:00 P.M., and 10:00 P.M. Depending on the species and age, the chicks took 1.1 to 1.4 ounce (30–40 g) of formula. An average seven-to-eight day-old chick, weighing 4.4 ounces (125 g) when taken from the nest, gained about 2.4 ounces (68 g) after one week, in the second week an additional 1.06 to 1.13 ounce (30–32 g), and in the third week about 0.92 to 0.99 ounce 26–28 g).

When they reach two to three months of age and are fully feathered, most *Pionus* species have the habit of making a wheezing noise at feeding time, or when they are hungry; they almost seem to have a respiratory problem. This behavior is unique to this group of birds, but it will do no harm (yes, I would rather take no risks!) to have them examined by an avian veterinarian.

Hand-feeding Finches

Newly hatched young must be fed first after about 12 hours with a very thin mixture of commercial hand-feeding diet. At this stage the

A breeding pair of Mitchell's Lories (**Trichoglossus ornatus mitchelli**).

yolk sac is clearly visible on the abdomen of the baby bird. Tube-feeding should be done with a shortened red catheter attached to a small syringe. If the chick won't open its mouth, a light tap on the beak often will help. Weak birds must usually be helped the first few times. You can open the beak by lifting the upper mandible with the end of the tube. Take care not to overfeed when the yolk sac is still

A young Blue and Gold Macaw, hand-fed and raised by the author.

For the first four days, the birds should be fed at two hourly intervals, starting at 6:00 A.M. and finishing at midnight, with an extra feeding at 3:00 A.M. I mix 1 cc Pedialyte (a human baby preparation with electrolytes and sugars intended to combat dehydration) into the commercial food. After the fifth day I leave the 3:00 A.M. feeding out. The midnight feeding is offered with a bent spoon, and from the seventh day, three feedings with a bent spoon. From the ninth day all feedings are given via the spoon. The birds are now big enough to accept food directly into their mouths. A small plastic pipette can be used instead of a bent spoon if you feel more comfortable with that method. The spoon-feeding formula consists of commercial rearing food (such as CéDé), moistened with enough water to make it easy for the young to swallow. From the ninth day the birds are given soaked and sprouted seeds (millet, canary seed, etc.), as well as millet spray. They are gradually introduced to harder seeds, greens, and pieces of cuttlebone. Look in the literature for the diets of the various species.

Hand-feeding Mynahs

Over the years I have hand-raised the following mynah species: the Lesser Indian Hill Mynah, *Gracula religiosa indica*; the Greater Indian Hill Mynah, *G. r. intermedia*, and the Java Mynah, *G. r. religiosa*. In The

visible. The baby bird's skin is translucent so it is easy to see when the tube is in the crop. Go carefully (the crop is very fragile) and especially not so "deep" that you can't see what you're doing. Carefully depress the plunger. Try to stop food from coming out of the crop into the mouth. If this should happen, hold the chick upside down and wipe the beak clean with a tissue. Give the bird a little time to recover before proceeding.

Netherlands I hand-reared some Rothschilds Mynahs, *Leucospar rothschildi* (in The Netherlands a number of aviculturists specialize in the breeding of this species); the Common or Bank Mynah, *Acridotheres tristis*; and the Pagoda Mynah, *Sturnus pagodarum*.

All species were hand-fed in a similar manner. From the first to fifth days the young of the above species were fed with very small pieces of day-old mice. The pieces of meat were mixed in a water solution of vitamin/mineral preparation to prevent dehydration. They were fed every 45 minutes from 7:00 A.M. to midnight. From the fifth day they were given little balls of moistened mynah pellets, mixed with some rearing food (CéDé or similar product), ground insects, and a vitamin/mineral preparation. Gradually, the feeds were reduced to hourly, then every two hours. The food was given with a wooden spatula. Depending on the species, the birds can be placed in a cage after two to three weeks, and the feeds can be reduced to every three hours. Once in the cage, the babies soon showed interest in food offered in a shallow dish and began to take small pieces of food themselves, but if they saw me approaching, they would still open their beaks, flutter their wings, and beg for food. Before I began to hand-feed I placed the bird on the table, took a little food in my fingers, and offered it to the bird. The birds usually reacted positively to this and readily accepted the food from my fingers. Then I returned to the normal

A young Scarlet Macaw (Ara macao), hand-fed and raised by the author.

hand-feeding. At three weeks to one month old, the birds were more or less independent, feeding themselves from the bowl (see page 113), although for the first week I took care to be sure that they were eating enough food. I checked them particularly, about one hour before they went to sleep, to be sure that the crop was full; if less than half-full, they were hand-fed.

Chapter Nine
Health Problems

Introduction

Sick birds, or birds that have been injured (usually our fault—burned crop, for example) should be taken to an avian veterinarian, or you should at least consult one by phone if it is not possible to visit for one reason or another. The following avian diseases and conditions are arranged in alphabetical order for your convenience.

Diseases, Symptoms, and Treatments

Aspiration

Aspiration is caused by the inhalation of fluid or thin formula into the lungs via the trachea. When the bird is feeding under normal circumstances, the trachea is closed off. If it accidentally opens during feeding, for one reason or another, food can get into the lungs. It also may happen if the crop is too full. A small amount of fluid in the trachea will cause the bird to cough, sneeze, and shake its head; sometimes food even comes out of the nostrils. Food or fluid in the lungs will cause respiratory difficulties, accompanied by clicking or rasping sounds. Without help, the bird will either die, or pneumonia will set in. In the latter case, the bird will die after several hours or days. Consult an avian veterinarian immediately if aspiration occurs.

Aspergillosis

This is caused most frequently by the fungus *Aspergillus fumigatus*, the airborne spores of which can infect humans as well as animals. *Aspergillus* species are most at home in a stuffy, moist, and warm atmosphere. Damp, dirty nest material or substrate materials are often a source of the fungus. The spores often enter the respiratory tract and cause problems. The eyes can also be affected and the bird will often hold its head to one side. Strict hygienic measures are required to control this fungus, including the frequent and routine cleaning of all cages, brooders, utensils, etc., as well as the frequent changing of all soiled and moist substrate materials.

Bacterial Diseases

Bacteria are single-celled plant-like organisms that usually reproduce asexually, by cell division. Bacteria occur in the millions throughout the atmosphere. There are many harmless bacteria, as well as those that cause disease. Diseases may be caused by the bacteria themselves, or by the toxins that they produce as by-products. It is important to know which organism causes which disease, so that the correct treatment can follow.

A sick bird is first examined externally for symptoms and/or ectoparasites. The feces can be examined for endoparasites. If a bird dies, a necropsy will usually reveal the cause of death by microscopically locating the particular causative bacteria and cultivating them for a few days. Once a diagnosis is reached, the necessary treatments for further cases can be decided.

Salmonellosis: This occurs among birds as well as among other kinds of animals and humans. It is particularly common in doves and canaries, less so in parrots and parakeets. The most important salmonella species in birds is *Salmonella typhimurium*. Salmonella bacteria can be transmitted to healthy birds from sick birds, or even birds that are not apparently sick but are "carriers" of the disease (known as the "latent form" of the disease). The disease can be caught from travel baskets, transport boxes, droppings, saliva, and crop milk, and can even be passed, through the oviduct, to the egg. Flies, rats, and mice are also often responsible for spreading the disease, by con-

Your avian veterinarian plays a very important part in your hobby!

taminating food or drinking water. Salmonella bacteria can live for up to 18 months in the host, or up to six weeks in a corpse.

Salmonellosis can be acute in many cage and aviary birds. The incubation time of the disease is four to five days, after which the first symptoms will appear. A sick bird often mopes in a corner with its feathers fluffed out, and it loses the strength to feed. The cloaca is usually soiled with droppings that are greenish and watery. The disease can spread from the intestines through the bloodstream and affect other internal organs. Sometimes there are breathing difficulties caused when the disease attacks the lungs. In pigeons the disease is sometimes called "twisting neck disease," but is usually called *paratyphus*. There are three forms of the disease:

1. *The Organ Form*. The intestines are infected and the bird passes slimy, greenish brown colored feces. The bird may drink more but eat less and lose weight. It will become lethargic, fluff out its feathers, and lose interest in its surroundings. Frequently the liver, heart, and kidneys are also infected. An infected female can pass the disease through the oviduct to the embryo. These usually die in the egg after about ten days.

2. *The Joint Form*. The Salmonella bacteria infect the joints, through the bloodstream. The joints swell and stiffen. Mostly one, sometimes both, wings are affected. The feet are often affected, causing crippling.

3. *The Nerve Form*. The bacteria invade the nerves and spinal cord, causing loss of balance and general debilitation. The bird shakes its head and becomes disoriented. Eventually, the bird will be unable to feed or drink.

Birds infected with Salmonellosis must be immediately isolated and treated with appropriate antibiotics. Intravenous fluid therapy may be necessary to correct dehydration. All infected cages and utensils must be thoroughly disinfected. Consult an avian veterinarian immediately.

Pseudotuberculosis: This is caused by the bacillus *Yersinia pseudotuberculosis* and may occur in many bird species, but especially canaries and other songbirds, as well as in many psittacines. The disease can be transmitted by wild birds, rats, and mice contaminating food or drinking water. Stressed birds are especially prone to the disease. The incubation time is three to six days and spreads through the mucous membranes in the nostrils, the buccal cavity, and the esophagus, after which the spleen and liver can be affected. They swell up, and the bird has difficulty breathing. The main symptoms are lethargy, loss of weight, and sometimes diarrhea. Sudden death is most common and can occur within a week after symptoms appear.

To minimize the possibilities of an outbreak of pseudotuberculosis, birds should not be stressed. Rodents must be kept away from aviaries and birdrooms (strict rodent control). Infected birds must be isolated and an avian veterinarian should be consulted. The birds can be treated with antibiotics.

Colibacillosis: This disease is caused by the bacillus *Escherichia coli* and can soon infect an entire stock of nestling birds kept in unhygienic conditions. The disease is spread through the droppings of infected birds or other animals contaminating the food or water. It manifests itself in intestinal disorders that cause diarrhea, especially dangerous in the nest as the fluid droppings can no longer be removed by the parents and the bacteria can quickly multiply in the moist warmth of the nest. The bacteria can even encroach into the yolk sac of young nestlings, through the navel.

Infected nestlings have no will to beg for food and quickly lose weight. An entire nest of youngsters can easily be lost to this disease, but the parents have a better chance of overcoming it. The disease can be diagnosed only by bacterial examination.

After consulting your avian veterinarian, carefully sponge down the affected nestlings with warm water. The diarrhea must be stopped as soon as possible to prevent dehydration. All infected cages and utensils must be thoroughly disinfected, and disposable materials preferably burned. The birds should be transferred to a clean, isolated cage. The veterinarian will probably prescribe antibiotic treatment.

Necrotic enteritis: Sometimes known as quail disease, this is especially common among youngsters of the Japanese Quail, *Coturnix coturnix japonica,* and the Bob-white Quail, *Colinus virginianus.* It also occurs to a lesser extent in chickens, pheasants, partridges, doves, and other birds. The causative organism is *Clostridium colinum,* which affects the small intestine and the appendix. The bacteria are anerobic, meaning that they can live without oxygen. The toxins produced by these organisms attack the walls of the intestines and destroy their ability to pass nutrients into the bloodstream. The liver and spleen are also affected. Symptoms include thin, bloody feces and loss of appetite. Dehydration, coupled with lack of nutrition, can lead to death in a few days.

As there are several diseases with similar symtoms, necrotic enteritis is hard to diagnose. You should immediately consult an avian veterinarian if any of the above symptoms appear in your birds. Only bacterial examination of the feces of living birds, or dissection on dead birds, will give a positive diagnosis. Effective antibiotics include penicillin and virginiamycin. Sick birds must be immediately isolated from other stock. Be sure they have adequate water to combat dehydration, give easily digestible food and extra vitamin A for a week, remove feces daily, and take the usual intensive disinfection measures.

(Avian) Tuberculosis: The causative organism is *Mycobacterium avium*, in parrots also *M. bovius* and *M. tuberculosis*. This chronic disease mainly affects the digestive system. It is difficult to diagnose the disease in the living bird, but rapid weight loss is one of the symptoms. Consult your avian veterinarian immediately if this happens.

Dissection of a dead bird will show wasting of the breast muscles and lack of subcutaneous and abdominal fat. Many of the organs will exhibit whitish yellow papillae up to 10 mm in diameter. The liver, spleen, lungs, air sacs, and intestines are the main organs infected. The liver and spleen are often larger than normal, brittle, and greenish in color.

The causative organism can live for years in bird accommodations, so frequent and regular disinfection of all cages, utensils, and surfaces is the main method of control.

Other, less frequent bacterial diseases include:

Listeriosis: This is caused by *Listeria monocytogenes*. The bird may be treated with antibiotic.

Streptococcal infections: These can be transmitted by the red bird mite, *Dermanyssus gallinae.* Overcrowding, dampness, and poor hygiene will encourage the outbreak of this disease.

Staphylococcal infections: These can be caused by several species, including *Staphylococcus aureus* and *S. albus*. The disease is often present in imported parrots. Stress can influence the development of both streptococcal and staphylococcal infections and can lead to fatalities. Wounds and/or insect bites should be treated to prevent access to the germs. Paint such wounds with mercurochrome, or iodine to combat infection. Treatment of staphylococcus is with specific therapy as determined by sensitivity and culture testing.

Beak Deformities

It's not always the faulty use of feeding utensils that causes beak deformities; faulty growth of the skull bones can also be to blame. When such deformities are noticed at an early stage, and the beak is still malleable, they can often be corrected by gentle manipulation. The upper mandible is gripped along its sides with thumb and forefinger, close to the tip, but not as far back as the nostrils. With the same fingers of the other hand, the tip of the beak is gently pressed into position, that is to say, with the edges of the upper mandible lined up over the edges of the lower mandible. Hold in this position for five to seven seconds, then release and repeat the procedure. This therapy should be repeated for two minutes, five to eight times a day.

Another possibility is the growth of the lower mandible over the upper in a slanting position. In such a situation, the lower mandible can be carefully filed down before repeating the therapy described above. Should you feel uncomfortable doing this, it is best to consult an avian veterinarian.

Candidiasis

This fungus disease is caused by the yeast, *Candida albicans*. The spores thrive on the tongue, in the pharynx, the upper digestive tracts (including the esophagus), the proventriculus, the ventriculus, the lower intestinal tract (especially the duodenum, the first part of the small intestine, connecting with the outlet of the gizzard) and, occasionally, on the skin, eyes, beak, lungs, and air sacs. Candidiasis occurs mainly in birds that:
• are fed a monotonous diet;

- are fed with an easily fermentable diet;
- are, or have been, subjected to a protracted course of antibiotic treatment.

Fatalities from this infection usually occur first in young birds.

Foods that ferment readily include rearing food (egg food, universal food) and germinated seeds that are not replaced in time. Lory and lorikeet diet and other softbill food will easily ferment if faultily prepared or stored for too long. Rearing formula that is too dry will cause crop compaction, also often leading to candidiasis. Long courses of antibiotics (as often given to newly imported psittacines in quarantine) can destroy the natural normal flora in a bird's intestines and allow the *Candida* to multiply out of proportion. There are no specific symptoms of the disease, but digestive problems and loss of appetite and weight frequently occur.

Treatment consists of administration of an antifungal medicine. You can also add 0.5 gram (0.02 fl. oz.) of copper sulphate per liter (1.06 qt.) of drinking water, and give the birds extra vitamin A. Only easily digestible food, such as germinated seed, soft food, or liquid formula should be given. Avian veterinarians often use one of the following medicines to treat the disease: Mycostatin (Nystatin), Flucystosine (Ancoban) (both are antifungal drugs); Amphotericin-B lotion and Amphotericin-B ointment (for topical use in the mouth and eyes respec-

tively); *Lactobacillus* (to reestablish the normal intestinal flora); and Levamisole (an immune system stimulant). Chlorhexadane (Novassan) is often added to the drinking water, but the dilutions should be strictly as advised by a veterinarian. The drug can also be added to the baby hand-feeding formula.

Clogged Cloaca (Pseudocoprostosis)

Dried feces around the cloaca can make it difficult or impossible for a baby bird to pass feces. The area should be swabbed clean with warm water or mineral oil. If the inside of the cloaca is clogged (hard, dry fecal plugs can often be seen through the skin of the abdomen), use a small cotton-tipped swab lubricated with petroleum jelly and insert it gently into the cloaca, to release the plug.

Clogged Nostrils

Dust, food particles, or bedding can clog the nostrils. Use a blunt toothpick or matchstick to gently remove the obstacle, then flush with a little saline or warm water, using a plastic eyedropper. The bird will usually sneeze and cough during treatment, but there is no need to worry about this.

Conjunctivitis

This is an infection of the membranes lining the upper and lower eyelids that can be caused by foreign matter accidentally getting into the eye of the baby bird. In older birds it is a consequence of a viral infection, such as avian pox. The eyelids are often pasted shut by the discharge. As the eyes are very delicate and can stand little or no "experimentation," it is best to consult an avian veterinarian who will probably prescribe treatment with a broad spectrum ophthalmic antibiotic ointment. Fungi can also irritate the eye membranes; *Ketoconazol* and similar, more advanced ointments are the correct medications for this condition. Viral eye problems are best handled by the veterinarian.

Sealed or partly sealed eyelids caused by discharge should be first wiped clean with a warm compress, then gently pushed apart with the thumb and index finger (which you will first, of course, have disinfected!). During and after treatment, it is strongly recommended that extra vitamin A be administered in the drinking water.

Constipation

Failure to defecate can be caused by too dry a formula or dehydration. Moisten a small cotton-tipped swab with mineral oil and gently insert this into the cloaca. When you withdraw the swab, the obstruction should come loose. If the blockage is situated higher up, you should seek the assistance of an avian veterinarian, as such a condition can be life threatening. The diet must, of course, be improved to prevent the situation from repeating itself.

Crop Problems

Pendulous crop: In this condition the crop is stretched beyond its natural elastic property, usually the result of overfeeding. Birds like macaws, the larger conure species, and *Pionus* species (e.g., White-crowned Pionus), are especially prone to this condition at two to four weeks of age if overfed. It can result in the crop losing most or all of its natural elasticity, resulting in the food remaining in the crop for too long and turning sour (sour crop) or other digestive problems. It is best to take the bird to an avian veterinarian to have the crop corrected by removing part of the crop wall.

Crop burns: These occur if food is given too hot, often resulting in burn damage to the linings of the esophagus and crop. Blistering skin, scabs, and even perforation of the crop wall and skin can result. An avian veterinarian should be consulted immediately if this happens, even though small burns often heal themselves.

Sour crop: If food stays in the crop for too long, for one reason or another, it will ferment and turn sour and/or become hard (*crop impaction*). Crop impaction even occurs in adult birds that, for example, eat too much grit or swallow a foreign object. A crop that no longer functions, as if it were static, is known as *crop stasis*. This only occurs in adult birds and is caused by bacterial or fungal infections, usually as a result of eating spoiled food.

To avoid sour crop, it is absolutely essential that the crop has a chance to empty completely at least once in a 24-hour period (the last hand-feeding at midnight and first morning feed at 7:00 A.M. will give the crop seven hours to empty). The formula must, of course, always be correctly made up so that it is not the cause of fermentation.

Treatment for sour crop is as follows:

For young birds under one week old give one drop of Kaopectate or Pepto-Bismol every three hours; chicks one to two weeks old, two to four drops every three hours; chicks older than three weeks, two to four drops every two hours.

Chicks with crop impaction can be helped by giving one to two drops of mineral oil in the mouth. Once the drops are in the crop, wait a few minutes then gently massage it to break up the obstruction. Then give the bird a few (up to 3) drops of Di-gel or Maalox. Repeat this process several times a day until the impaction is cured. The birds should be given an easily digestible diet for a few days, such as the formula given on page 93.

Many aviculturists empty the crop manually if the bird seems to be having difficulties. A feeding tube, mounted on a syringe or suction bulb, is passed into the crop and the contents aspirated. If you have never done this, it is advisable to get the help of an avian veterinarian or an experienced aviculturist. Be extremely careful not to puncture the esophagus or crop lining. If this should happen, you will see swelling and inflammation around the wound. In severe cases, it is possible for food to leave the crop through the wound and rest beneath the skin. Surgical intervention is the only way open!

Adult birds suffering from sour crop are treated as follows:

Table 11
Sour Crop Treatment

Birds the size of a:	Drops every four hours:
Zebra Finch	1
Parakeet	2–4
Cockatiel	3–5
Cockatoo	15–24 (1 cc)
Amazon	15–24 (1 cc)
Macaw	15–40 (2 cc)

Curved Toes and Splayed Legs

Occasionally, birds are born with most or all of their toes curved inward. Research has shown that this is not necessarily a genetic defect. Consult your veterinarian, although the problem will usually correct itself if the birds get a proper diet and are regularly helped to stand on their feet properly.

If chicks must stand on a slippery surface (for example the bottom of a glass aquarium or plastic container), it is possible that their legs will continually slide apart. Corrections must be made in the brooders' nest boxes and the like. A diet that is not balanced can also cause splayed legs. Position the legs in the correct position and tape them together above the ankles with medical tape. Do not forget to inspect them daily; young chicks grow rapidly so the situation must be continually revised. Fortunately, the treatment does not take long and the bird is usually "standing on its own two legs" within four to seven days. If possible, the patient should be placed in a small brooder. If you are unfamiliar with this procedure, it is best to consult an avian veterinarian.

Dehydration

Young birds rarely suffer from dehydration if their formula is correctly prepared. Obviously, the brooder environment is equally important in younger altricial species. Birds with crop stasis, however, can quickly succumb to dehydration. When dehydrated, the skin of young birds becomes dark red instead of pink. If you pinch the skin, the color lightens only slightly on the part you pinch. Administer the formula given on page 93 and consult an avian veterinarian who (especially if the crop is not working properly) will give the bird a subcutaneous injection of lactated Ringer's solution.

Discolored and Deformed Feathers

A shortage of vitamin A, and of the amino acid (protein) lysine, are often the cause of feather development problems (birds that are fed exclusively on sunflower seed always end up with very bad plumage, or even with no plumage at all!) With correct nutrition, the birds will develop healthy, well-formed, colorful, sleek plumage after their first molt. If this is not the case, and the feathers grow out of the shafts in a twisted, frayed condition, it is possible that the bird is suffering from Psittacine Beak and Feather Disease, a viral disease that, at the present time, affects mainly parrotlike birds. Birds infected with the polyoma virus also may grow malformed feathers. In both cases the birds must be immediately isolated and an avian veterinarian consulted.

Lacerations of the Skin

In mild cases, treatment with an antibacteral ointment will suffice to treat these but, in severe cases, you should consult an avian veterinarian. Chicks occasionally bite each other in the legs or toes, or wounds may be caused by unsuitable bedding. Bleeding wounds should be immediately treated with a coagulating agent, and lightly dabbed with mineral oil. If there is suddenly a lot of blood, it can have been caused by broken blood feathers. Apply pressure to the injured feather shaft and treat with a coagulating agent. It is best to have an avian veterinarian remove the injured shaft.

Lethargy

If a young bird becomes listless, sluggish, and indifferent, it is said to be lethargic (the word is derived from the Latin *lethargia*, which means drowsiness). The bird must be kept under close observation. Admittedly, baby parrots are not the most active little beasts, but after a few weeks this situation will certainly change! Lethargic birds are simply slow at feeding time (or don't react at all to your efforts) and show no interaction with their siblings or with the breeder. In many cases it is a good idea to check the temperature in the brooder and adjust as necessary. If a chick is lethargic, it is advisable to check the droppings and make some gram stains or cultures to find out if the cause is a fungal or bacterial infection.

Malnutrition

This is caused by extremely poor nutrition due to an insufficient or poorly balanced diet, or because of defective digestion or defective utilization of foods. Young birds suffering from chronic malnutrition are easy to recognize—they are thin and have, in relation to the body, a big head and thin legs. The feathers are dull and frayed.

First, take a look at the formula: Why is it not accepted? Can we offer additional foods to improve the diet and bird? And—very importantly—is malnutrition apparent in others of the same species?

It is strongly recommended that you know your chicks through and through and are familiar with their appearance. Chicks of the same species more or less resemble each other but there are big differences among chicks of different species when compared with each other. Before deciding that a chick is suffering from malnutrition, it is important that you know what the chick *should* look like. If you have never before hand-reared a particular species, it is essential to have a look at the chicks of fellow aviculturists, and familiarize yourself with their appearance.

Poisoning

Consult *New Pet Bird Handbook* and *The Parrot in Health and Illness*, for a list of many indoor and outdoor plants that are poisonous to (baby) birds (see page 143). It goes without saying that birds must never come into contact with such plants. Even avocados and (large quantities of) parsley should not be given. High salt intake must be avoided in order to avoid heart disease and stroke. Cuttlebone collected at the beach must therefore be soaked for several hours in clean tapwater so that most of the salt dissolves; the water should be changed several times. The cuttlebone must then be dried out before it is given to the birds.

Important note: For years, avicultural writers have warned of the dangers of Teflon poisoning. Overheating of the Teflon (or similar products, such as Silverstone) coating on pans and other kitchen utensils is likely to kill birds. The gas released by the overheating is highly poisonous. Ban all Teflon coated utensils from your nursery!

A young African Gray Parrot.

Birds, and especially young birds, are very sensitive to harmful fumes from paint, cleaning materials, insecticides, kerosine heaters, gas stoves, furnaces, wood-burning stoves, and so on.

Medicines must also be used with great care. What may be harmless to adult birds can be toxic to young ones that come into contact with it. Beware especially of vermicides and the drug Mebendazole.

Molds and fungi can produce toxic substances called *myotoxins*. Peanuts may contain *aflatoxin*, a toxin that is responsible for destroying liver tissues and that may act as a potent cancer-causing agent (Burgmann). Various bacteria can also cause similar problems.

Glossary

Albumen The white of an egg; the substance existing in a nearly pure state in egg white, and constituting an element of animal solids and plants.

Albumin Any of a class of water-soluble proteins in animal and vegetable juices and tissues (meat, milk, eggs).

Botulinum (Botulinus) An anaerobic, rod-shaped bacterium (*Clostridum botuinum*) that secretes botulin and inhabits soils.

Botulism A disease of the nervous system caused by a toxin developed in spoiled foods.

Chlamydia An obligate intercellular organism causing Ornithosis (Psittacosis). It can be particularly virulent in unhygienic, stuffy, overcrowded conditions, as is exemplified by its high rate in imported birds, especially in those that have been smuggled.

Cloaca In birds (also in reptiles and certain fishes), the cavity receiving the discharges from intestinal, urinary, and generative canals.

Clutch A hatch of eggs; the eggs laid in one breeding attempt.

Coliform Of or pertaining to any of several bacilli, esp. *Escherichia coli* and members of the genus *Aerobater,* that are normally present in the colon and that indicate fecal contamination when found in the water supply.

Crop A pouchlike enlargement of the gullet of many bird species, in which food is held and softened.

Egg Binding The state of being unable to lay an egg that's ready to come out. The affected female bird looks sick, sits hunched up, and moves little. The most common causes are calcium deficiency and general malnutrition. Transfer the patient to a hospital cage and raise the temperature to about 90°F (32°C). Consult an avian veterinarian immediately.

Embryo An organism in the earliest stages of its development, as the young of a bird in the egg, or the young of a mammal in the womb.

Environment The aggregate of surrounding things, conditions, or influences. An environmentalist is any person who advocates or works to protect the air, water, and other natural resources from pollution.

Follicle A small cavity, sac, or gland.

Gallinaceous Birds Birds resembling the domestic fowls and pheasants such as grouse, quail, and turkeys.

Giardia Intestinal parasite in cage and aviary birds, especially in budgerigars (parakeets) and cockatiels.

Gullet The esophagus; a tube connecting the mouth with the stomach.

Hemoglobin The protein coloring matter of the red blood corpuscles that serves to convey oxygen to the tissues.

Hygrometer Any instrument for measuring the water-vapor content of the atmosphere.

Infundibulum Entrance of the oviduct where fertilization occurs soon after the release of the ovum.

Mycobacterium Any of the several rod-shaped aerobic bacteria of the genus *Mycobacterium,* of which certain species are pathogenic.

Mycoplasma Any of a group of very small microorganisms without cell walls, of the prokaryote class Mollicutes, that are a common cause of pneumonia and urinary tract infections.

Ornithology The branch of zoology that deals with birds. An ornithologist is a bird expert.

Ova; pl., of Ovum The germ or egg of a female animal.

Ovary Either of a pair of female reproductive glands in which ova are formed.

Oviduct The passageway (either of a pair of tubes) that carries the ova from the ovary to the exterior.

Oviparous Producing eggs that hatch after being expelled from the body.

Ovoviviparous Producing eggs that are hatched within the body, so that the young are born alive but without placental attachment, as certain fish and reptiles.

Ovulation The shedding of eggs from an ovary.

Papilla A small, nipplelike process or projection, as on the tongue or in the mouth corners of young finchlike birds.

Pathogen Any disease-producing organism.

Photoperiod The interval in a 24-hour period during which an organism is exposed to light.

Pigment Any substance that gives color to the tissues or cells of animals and plants.

Posterior Situated behind or at the rear.

Pseudomonas Genus of several rod-shaped bacteria.

Raptors Birds of prey, usually belonging to the order Falioniformes.

Regurgitation To surge or cause to surge back, as undigested food from the stomach.

Spermatozoa A mature male reproductive cell.

Staphylococcus Any of several spherical bacteria occurring in irregular clusters.

Uterus The organ of female mammals and birds in which the young or the eggs develop before birth.

Vagina The membranous canal leading from the uterus to the vulva in female mammals and birds.

Virus Any of a group of microscopic infectious agents that reproduce only in living cells and cause diseases.

Viviparous Bringing forth living young rather than eggs, as most mammals.

Yeast A yellowish, semifluid froth consisting of certain minute-celled fungi causing fermentation.

Yolk The yellow and principal substance of an egg.

Useful Literature and Addresses

Literature

Abramson, J., B. L. Speer, D.V.M., and J. B. Thomsen. *The Large Macaws.* Fort Bragg, California: Raintree Publications, 1995.

Anderson Brown, Dr. A. F.. *The Incubation Book.* Exeter, England: The World Pheasant Association, 1987.

Burgmann, Petra, D.V.M. *Feeding Your Pet Bird.* Hauppauge, New York: Barron's Educational Series, Inc., 1993.

Doane, B. Munro. *The Parrot in Health and Illness, An Owner's Guide.* New York: Howell Book House, 1991.

Jordan, R. *Parrot Incubation Procedures.* Ontario, Canada: Silvio Mattacchione and Co., Pickering, 1989.

Low, Rosemary. *Cockatoos in Aviculture.* London, England: Blandford Press, 1993.

———. *Hand-Rearing Parrots and Other Birds.* Poole, England: Blandford Press, 1987.

Raethel, Dr. Heinz-Sigurd. *The New Duck Handbook.* Hauppauge, New York: Barron's Educational Series, Inc., 1989.

Schubot, Richard M., Kevin J. Clubb, and Susan L. Clubb, D.V.M. *Psittacine Aviculture, Perspectives, Techniques and Research.* Loxahatchee, Flordia: Avicultural Breeding and Research Center, 1992.

Silva, Tony. *Psittaculture, The Breeding, Rearing & Management of Parrots.* Pickering, Ontario, Canada: Silvo Mattacchione and Co., 1991.

Steinigeweg, Werner, D.V.M. *The New Softbill Handbook.* Hauppauge, New York: Barron's Educational Series, Inc., 1988.

Stoodley, John and Pat: *Genus Amazona.* Portsmouth, England: Bezels Publications, 1990.

Voren, Howard, and Rich Jordan. *Parrots, Hand-feeding and Nursery Management.* Pickering, Ontario, Canada: Silvio Mattacchione and Co., 1992.

Vriends, Matthew M., Ph.D. *Breeding Cage and Aviary Birds.* New York: Howell Book House, 1985.

————. *Conures.* Hauppauge, New York: Barron's Educational Series, Inc., 1992.

————. *Doves.* Hauppauge, New York: Barron's Educational Series, Inc., 1994.

————. *Gouldian Finches.* Hauppauge, New York: Barron's Educational Series, Inc., 1991.

————. *Lories and Lorikeets.* Hauppauge, New York: Barron's Educational Series, Inc., 1993.

————. *Lovebirds.* Second Edition, Hauppauge, New York: Barron's Educational Series, Inc., 1995.

————. *Pigeons.* Hauppauge, New York: Barron's Educational Series, Inc., 1988.

————. *Simon & Schuster's Guide to Pet Birds.* New York, New York: Simon & Schuster, 8th printing, 1994.

————. *The New Australian Parakeet Handbook.* Hauppauge, New York: Barron's Educational Series, Inc., 1992.

————. *The New Canary Handbook.* Hauppauge, New York: Barron's Educational Series, Inc., 1992.

————. *The New Cockatiel Handbook.* Hauppauge, New York: Barron's Educational Series, Inc., 1989.

————. *The New Pet Bird Handbook.* Hauppauge, New York: Barron's Educational Series, Inc., 1989.

Brooders, Thermometers, Hygrometers, Hospital Cages, Purifiers, and Incubators

Cloud-9 Air Purifiers
  P.O. Box 5611
  Evanston, Ilinois
  Tel.: 1-800-242-7873

Dean's Animal Supply
  P.O. Box 691418
  Orlando, Florida 32869
  Tel.: 407-521-2963

D & M Bird Farm
  13585 Millpond Way
  San Diego, California 92129
  Tel.: 619-538-5544

Joe Feed's "Pet"istric Supply, Inc.
  1018 W. 63rd Street South
  Witchita, Kansas 67217
  Tel.: 316-524-1154

The Himidaire Incubator Company
  P.O. Box 9
  New Maidson, Ohio 45346-0009
  Tel.: 513-996-3001

Lyon Electric Company, Inc.
  2765 Main Street
  Chula Vista, California 91911
  Tel.: 619-420-1426

Pure Natural Systems
  5L-B Cummings Park
  Suite 311-B
  Woburn, Massachusetts 01801
  Tel.: 1-800-237-9199

RR Manufacturing Co.
  P.O. Box 1415
  Buffalo, Missouri 65622
  Tel.: 417-345-2200

Schaeffer Co.
  P.O. Box 217
  Moline, Illinois 61265
  Tel.: 309-762-6666

Hand-feeding Diets

Rolf C. Hagen (USA) Corp.
  P.O. Box 9107
  Mansfield, Massachusetts 02048
  Tel.: 1-800-225-2700 or 2701

Kaytee Products, Inc.
  P.O. Box 230
  Chilton, WI 53014
  Tel.: 1-800-669-9580

L/M Animal Farms
  10279 State Rte. 132
  Pleasant Plain, Ohio 45162
  Tel.: 513-877-2131

Pretty Bird International, Inc.
  5810 Stacy Trail
  Stacy, Minnesota 55079
  Tel.: 1-800-356-5020

Roudybush Diets
  Box 908
  Templeton, California 93465
  Tel.: 805-237-9991

Sunshine Bird Supplies
  8535 N.W. 56th Street
  Miami, Florida 33166
  Tel.: 305-593-2666

ZuPreem
  P.O. Box 2094
  Mission, Kansas 66202
  Tel.: 913-722-6336

Index

Color photos are indicated in **boldface** type.